This book is dedicated to the city of New York
and all the people who live in it.

NEW YORK

in photographs by

REINHART WOLF

TASCHEN

KÖLN LONDON MADRID NEW YORK PARIS TOKYO

preface
EDWARD ALBEE

text
SABINA LIETZMANN

interview
ANDY WARHOL

statements
Truman Capote, Le Corbusier, Henry James,
Philip Johnson, Lotte Lenya, Louise Nevelson,
Jean-Paul Sartre, Arthur Schlesinger jr.,
Diana Vreeland, Thomas Wolfe.

research
Office for Metropolitan History,
Christopher Gray, New York

Sabina Lietzmann "New York, die wunderbare Katastrophe": Courtesy Hoffmann und Campe Verlag, Hamburg;
Louise Nevelson "Dawns and Dusks": Courtesy Diana MacKown, Charles Scribner's Sons, New York.

NEW YORK! NEW YORK!

While I was growing up – or trying to – I lived at
home, with my mother, father and grandmother, some
twenty miles from New York City, in a splendid house on
the water. There were dogs and cats and cooks and
gardeners and cars, and, in the last, many trips to what was
called "the city".

And even now, when I am supposed to know better,
when I have travelled the world and seen its wonders (and
horrors), I still am apt, when I am asked – in Moscow, say, or
Tokyo – where I live, to say "in the city". I mean "in New
York", of course; I mean no disparagement of any other
metropolis; I am merely telling the name of my love and
my identity, and am amazed that not everyone knows at
once what I have meant.

As soon as I was old enough to be in the cars as they
headed toward "the city", I went along whenever I could. I
would beg for the front seat, to the right of either a parent
or the chauffeur, and I would gaze intently ahead of me,
eager for the first sighting of the towers, the minarets, the
ziggurats. I was an Emperor, you see; I was being driven to
my subjects, my capital; I had been away; I missed them
both; they both missed me.

I take it I was a fairly democratic Emperor – front seat,
and all – but, still, it was the most absolute of my childhood
fantasy-games. (Being kidnapped was my second most
absorbing fantasy, not that I encouraged it – indeed, I kept
a bow and arrow under my bed to fend off the kidnapper
when he slit the screen of my window and climbed into my
room – but it was a natural enough preoccupation if you
were a child growing up five miles from where the
Lindbergh baby had been recently stolen.)

The town; the towers, the minarets, the ziggurats; "the
city".

Is it odd that I can recall little of what being in "the
city" was like? I remember only the approach, and I dare
say leaving found me asleep, exhausted by the grandeur.
Only arriving: perhaps the tickertape, the swell of my
subjects, the royal banners obscured my view; or perhaps I
was whisked at once into a building – a marble and bronze
glory – for earth-shaking meetings.

It is said that we relate all related experiences to our
virgin one whether we want to or not – our last mistress (or
mister) to our first, our first Art of the Fugue with all subse-

quent ones – and so it is not surprising that the definition
of a city, as far as I am concerned, is New York.

(Would I have felt the same way had San Francisco or
Chicago been my kingdom? Perhaps: those who love those
cities most were born there – they and those who have
removed there from New York, happier with a less blinding
grail.)

I mention my childhood response to New York City
because I have not, in all the years, lost my enrapturement.
Each return is to the bed and body of a beloved, too
familiar yet ever new and surprising terrain.

My first trip to Europe was by propeller plane, my first
return by ship-steerage on an ancient Italian liner. I was
no Emperor now, even to myself, but I got to see the
kingdom from the sea. We came through the Verrazano
Narrows at dawn (or so my sense of the romantic tells me)
and, from as far bow-ward on the ship as I could get, I saw
the city rise. The twin nonsense of the World Trade Center
had not then risen to destroy the perfect arc of lower
Manhattan, and I was transfixed at the rail. I cried and I
laughed; I was nineteen and proud of the emotion.

For several years after – poorer even than then, city-
locked – I would take the ferry boat to Staten Island for the
journey back, to see Manhattan grow before me once again,
rise glistening in the mist, plunge upward from the seabed.
They have killed almost all the ocean liners now, and soon
the ferry boat will be all there is.

I am a wanderer: offer me a trip to a city, a country, and
I'm off. I wander for two reasons, I think – to learn new
things, and to come home. If they were to tell me I could
never leave New York again I would be dismayed, for I
would be bereft of the joy of return – though I would find
consolation in knowing that, begetting and absorbing, New
York is enough of the world to occupy any mind.

No wonder New York is disliked by the smug residents
of lesser cities; no wonder it is despised for all its accumu-
lations by those who possess too little to be reasonable. No
wonder – if you consider the wonder.

I have been poor in New York, and not poor; not poor is
better. Though – as curious as it may seem to some – how I
spend my time in this city of mine is not altered in
direction or intensity by money. The art galleries have always
been free; the museums either are or cost next to nothing;

one learned quickly how to sneak into concerts and plays;
one was never too poor to be able to steal a book or a
record one couldn't live (fully) without; the people – save a
not-so-precious few – have always been there for the asking,
and the stationary physical joys of the city – some of them
the subject of this book – don't turn their backs on the
hard-up.

New York is – who would question it? – all the things it
is said to be; ugly/beautiful; cold/embracing; destructive/
generative. Since nothing can be properly perceived except
in context and comparatively, who would want it any other
way?

I can sum up no "meaning" of New York. I am not good
at that sort of thing: I have always been better at questions
than conclusions.

Besides, I am a middle-aged kid living the reality of his
fantasy; and I suspect I will be at my discovery of "the city"
even when they have to wheel me down the streets.

Edward Albee
New York, May 1980

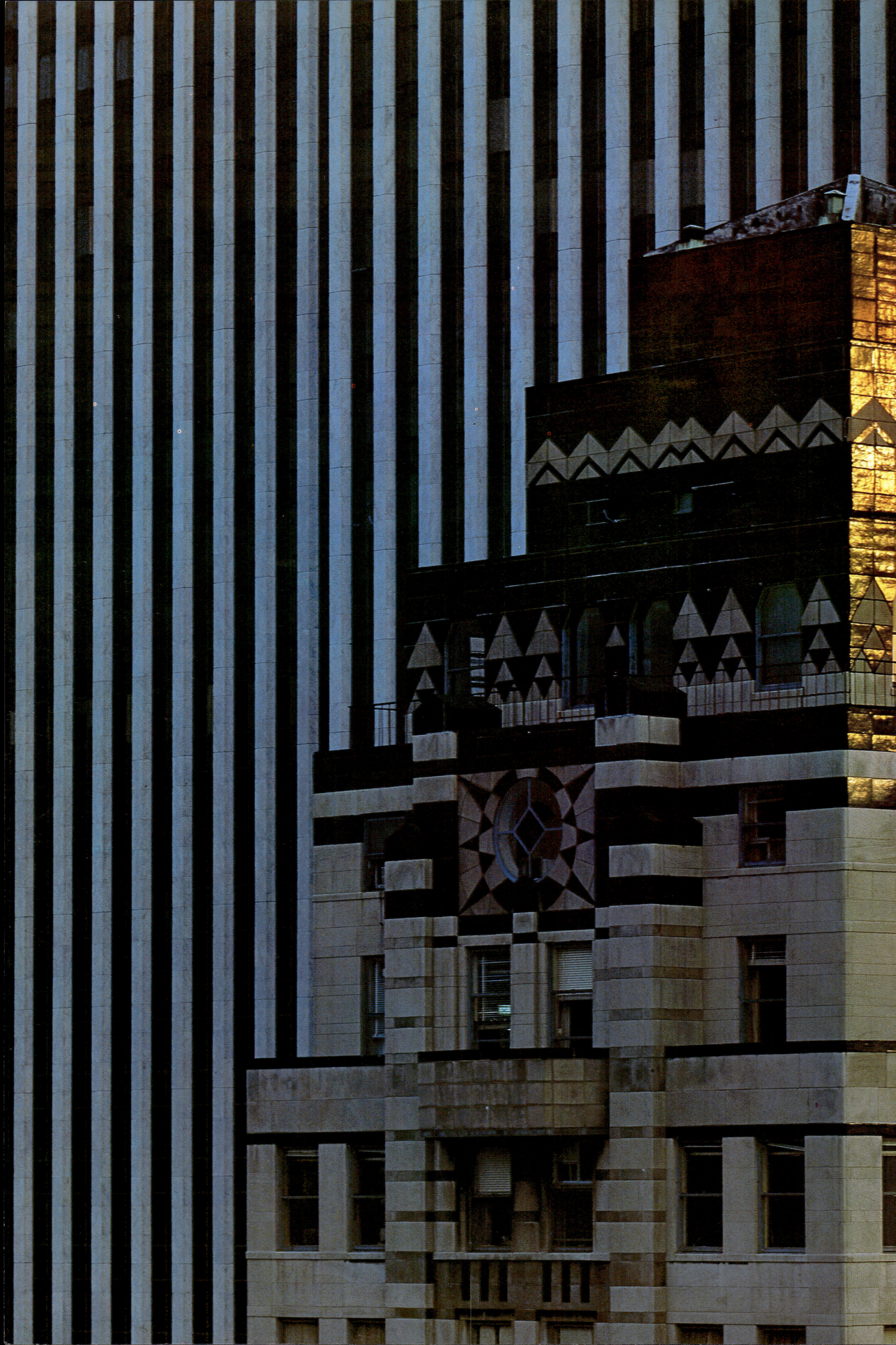

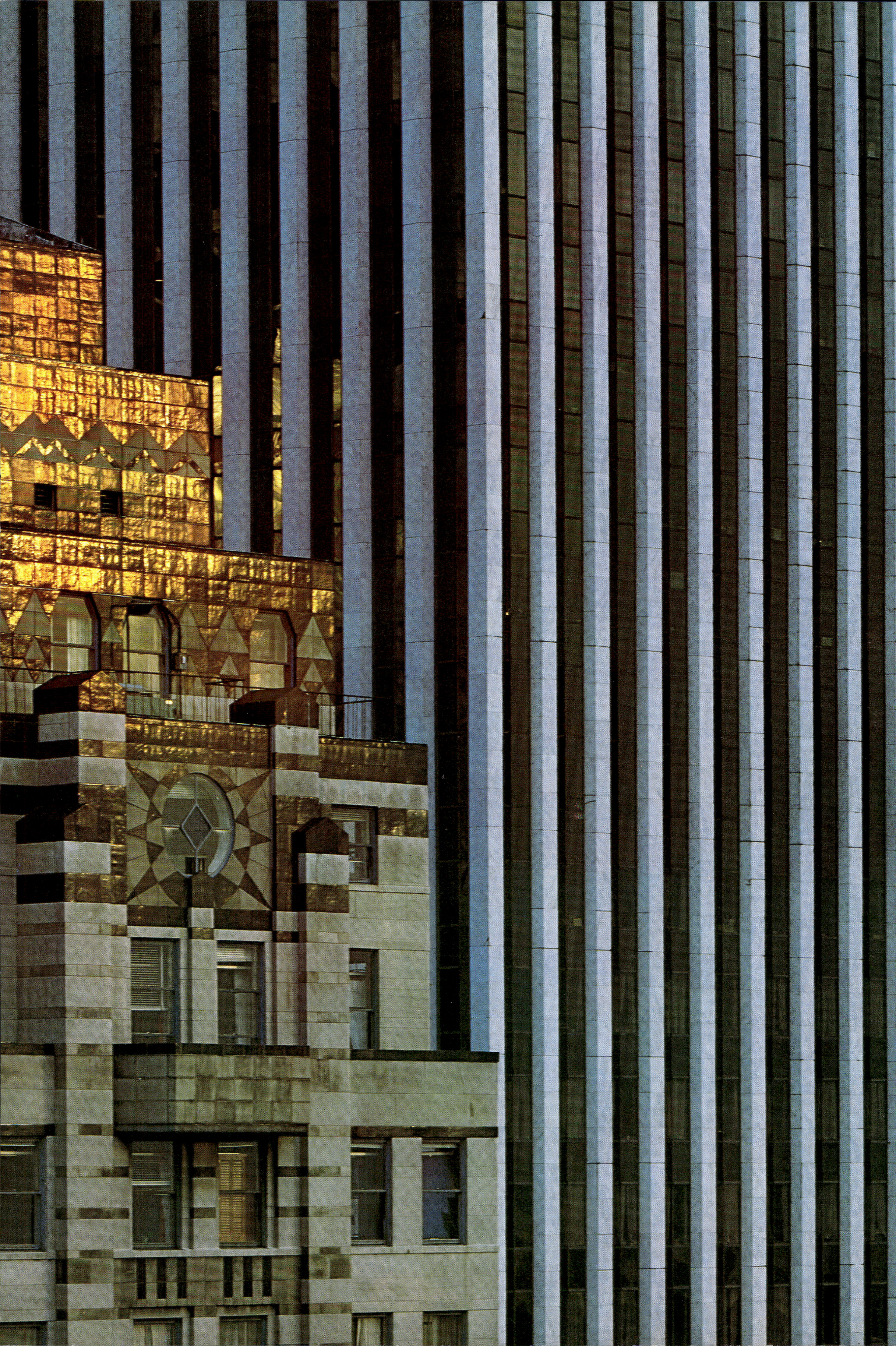

It's true what they say about New York: Life is cheap
out on its streets. People do get mugged in the parks in
broad daylight. Windows are barred and grated, doors are
locked, bolted, and locked again until many a New Yorker's
home is his fortress. The law of the jungle gnaws like some
malignant cancer at the vital organs of the city, threatens
the rule of law itself. An antiquated mass-transit system
does a better job torturing the city's masses than
transporting them. High-rise tenements pile up profits and
clutter the horizon. The air is pestilential. Ashes and acids
fall with the rain. Here is a city with the name Rockefeller
printed indelibly upon it – and rotting slums spread decay
till the cityscape is literally in ruins. All that is left of entire
neighborhoods "is what passed through them, the wind" –
Brecht's vision is already halfway realized. But only half, for
in the charred remains of the buildings the wind's old pals
have taken up lodgings – the killers, pickpockets, junkies
and pushers. New York, it would seem, stands under the
sentence of death – like Gomorrah, left to the wrath of God.

It's all true. And yet it is only a part of the truth – which
means it's untrue. New York is also the city great and high,
the city of pure gold, where dwell a proud and gladsome
people. New York is the New Jerusalem, the land of promise
and the city of praise where, as in the imperial cities of the
middle ages, people are set free. The Statue of Liberty in the
harbor is not some soul-stirring relic out of the past, not the
monument to war that we expect nations to erect. Emma
Lazarus's verses chiseled in the pedestal are still valid; there
the lady stands lifting her torch to light the way to golden
portals for the weary and persecuted, for the "huddled
masses yearning to breathe free". It is still a city of delive-
rance, an asylum for survivors, a promise of a myriad possibilities. The American saga goes on: even today the

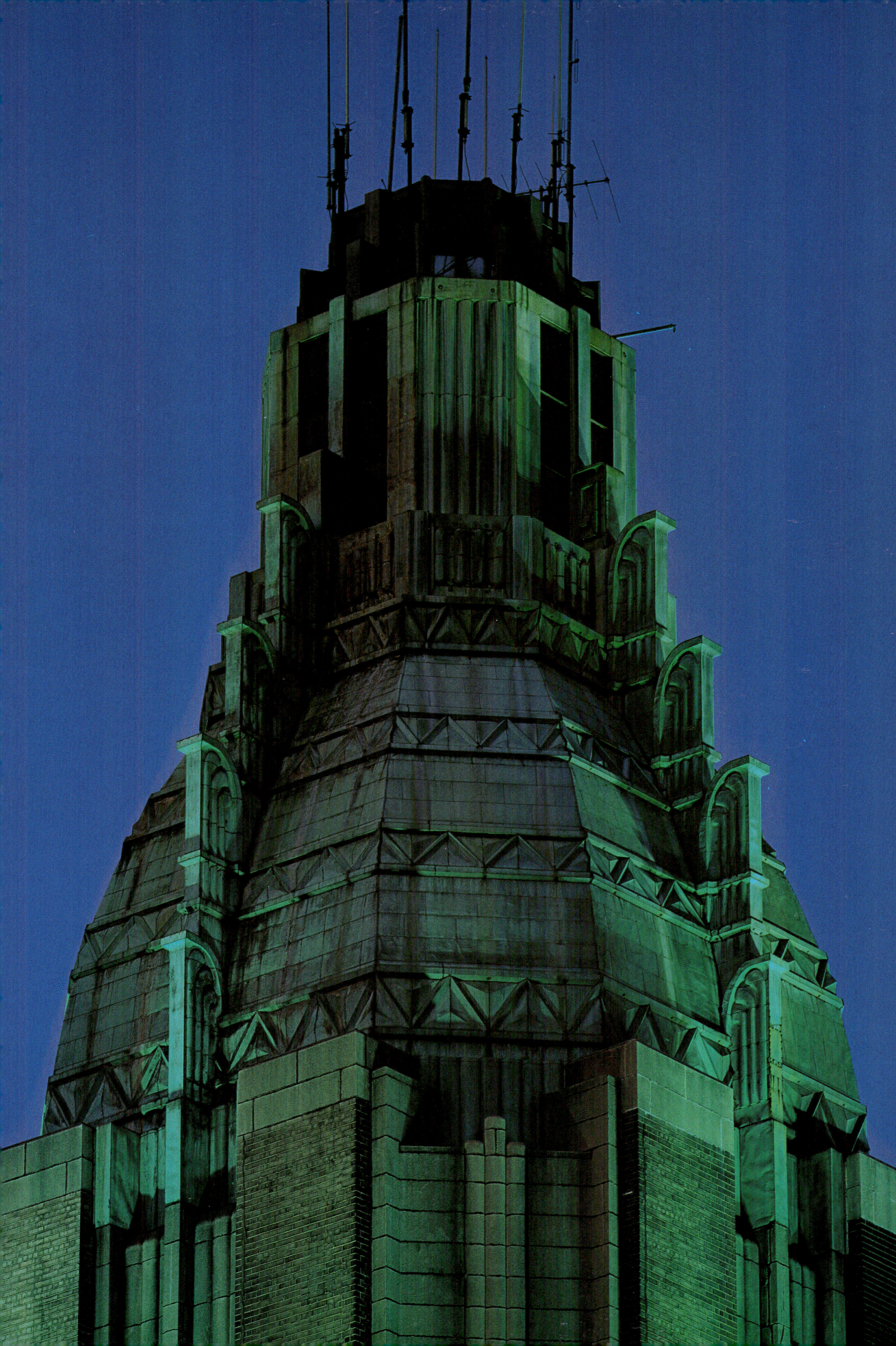

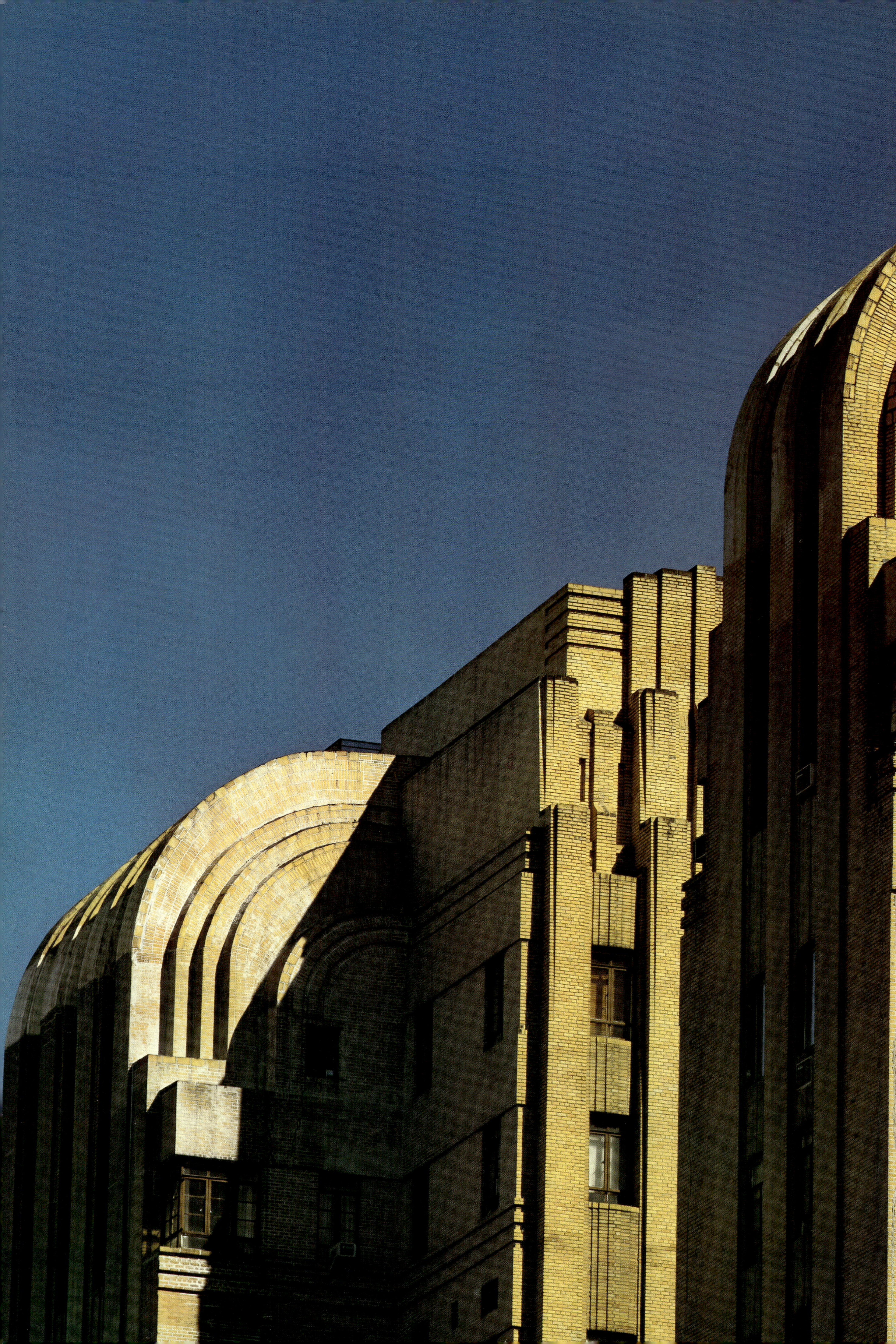

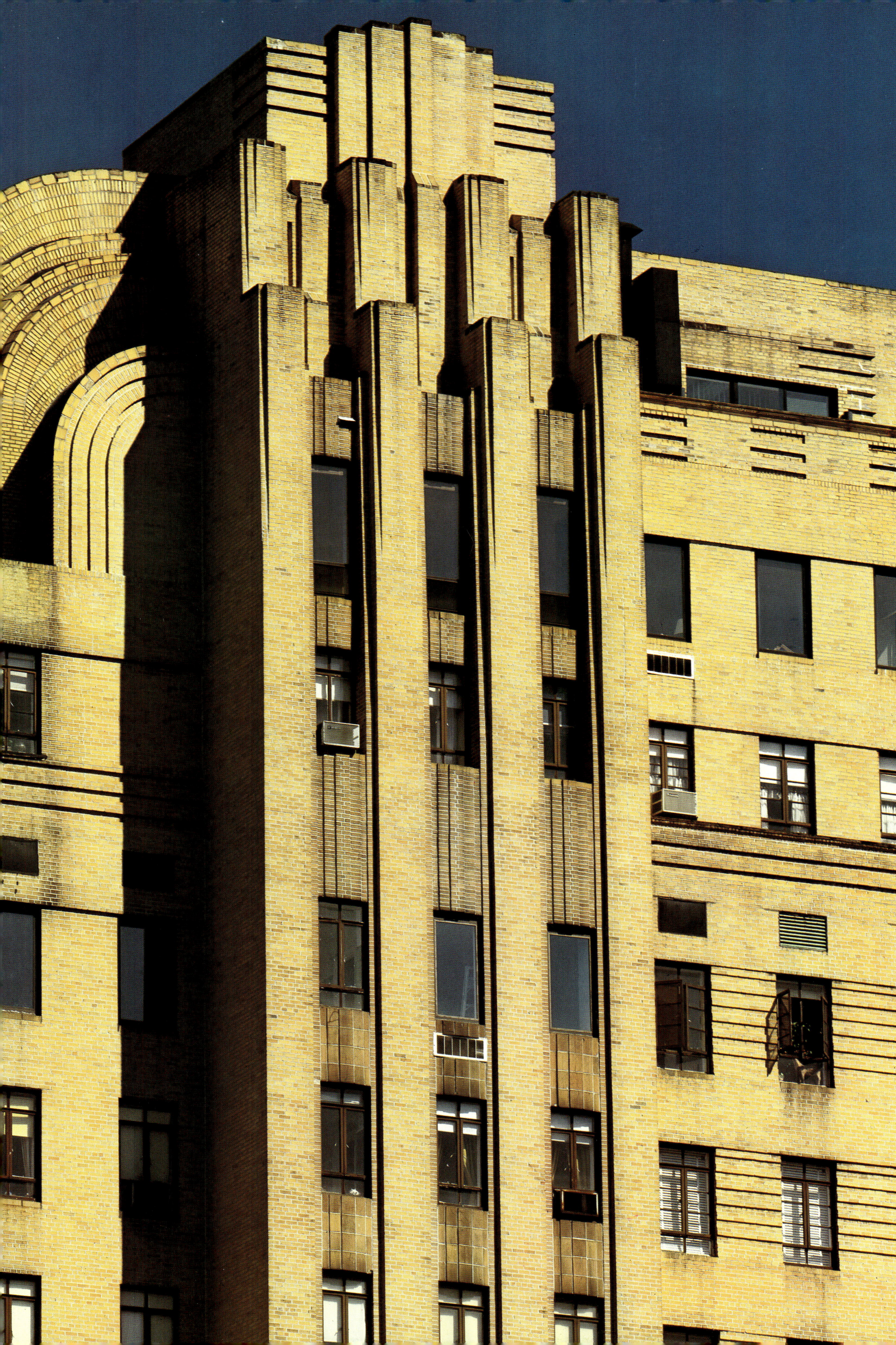

shoeshine boy can wind up his nation's ambassador to the United Nations, not two miles away from the corner where forty years before he would set up shop every morning. If you want to see New York, see it whole, you must see both sides, the scourge and the splendor, grappling with each other, bound to one another. New York is that beautiful and worthy catastrophe that Le Corbusier observed.

New York has a bad reputation in its own country. From Boston to Birmingham its citizens are pitied and mistrusted. The world beyond the city's borders takes a certain pleasure in its woes. Americans were told by one of their founding fathers, Thomas Jefferson, to distrust big cities and to see farms and rural life as the source of all virtue, and many of them still believe it today. The big city is a den of sin, corruption and wanton ways. And even the more urbane members of Congress, on whose generosity with public funds the cities are dependent to a considerable extent, even they regard New York as the Super-City doomed to perish of its own excess.

New York, it is said, is not America: one more half-truth. For the city is a great deal more provincial than it willingly admits. Iowa doesn't begin on the other side of the Hudson, as New Yorkers like to contend; middle-America is in fact very much at home just beyond Manhattan. The citizens of Brooklyn, Queens and Staten Island think much the same as do their compatriots in Kalamazoo or Phoenix. New York is, of course, the capital city – picked by no one, loved by few – the capital which determines America's tastes in culture, fashion, opinion and habits of consumption. And no one accepts decrees gladly and without opposition. But New York is also a research laboratory, the experimental station for new ideas, the national proving ground which spares others the risks. Whatever succeeds here benefits everyone – and no one else need suffer for the disasters. New York is Metropolis, everybody's guinea pig, the patient stretched out on the operating table while the doctors consult with one another whether an organism this size has any business being alive.

New York's achievements, however, are a feather in the cap for the whole country. In the vehement silhouette of Manhattan, in that vertical thrust which assaults heaven itself, America displays her power and self-confidence. Whoever has seen New York spread out below him across the night understands "why Americans have become proud of themselves and why they raise their voices in the world", as Le Corbusier has put it.

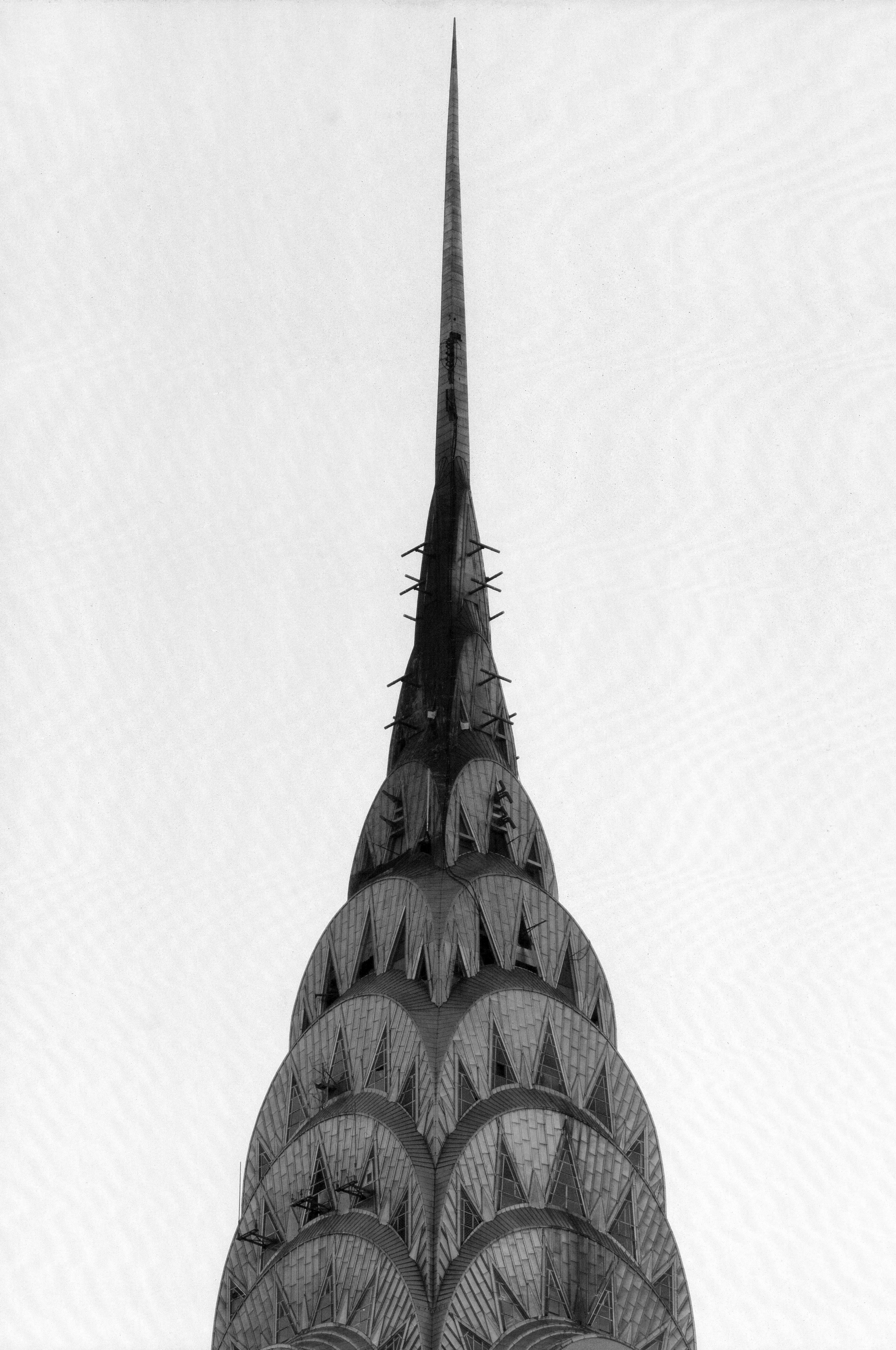

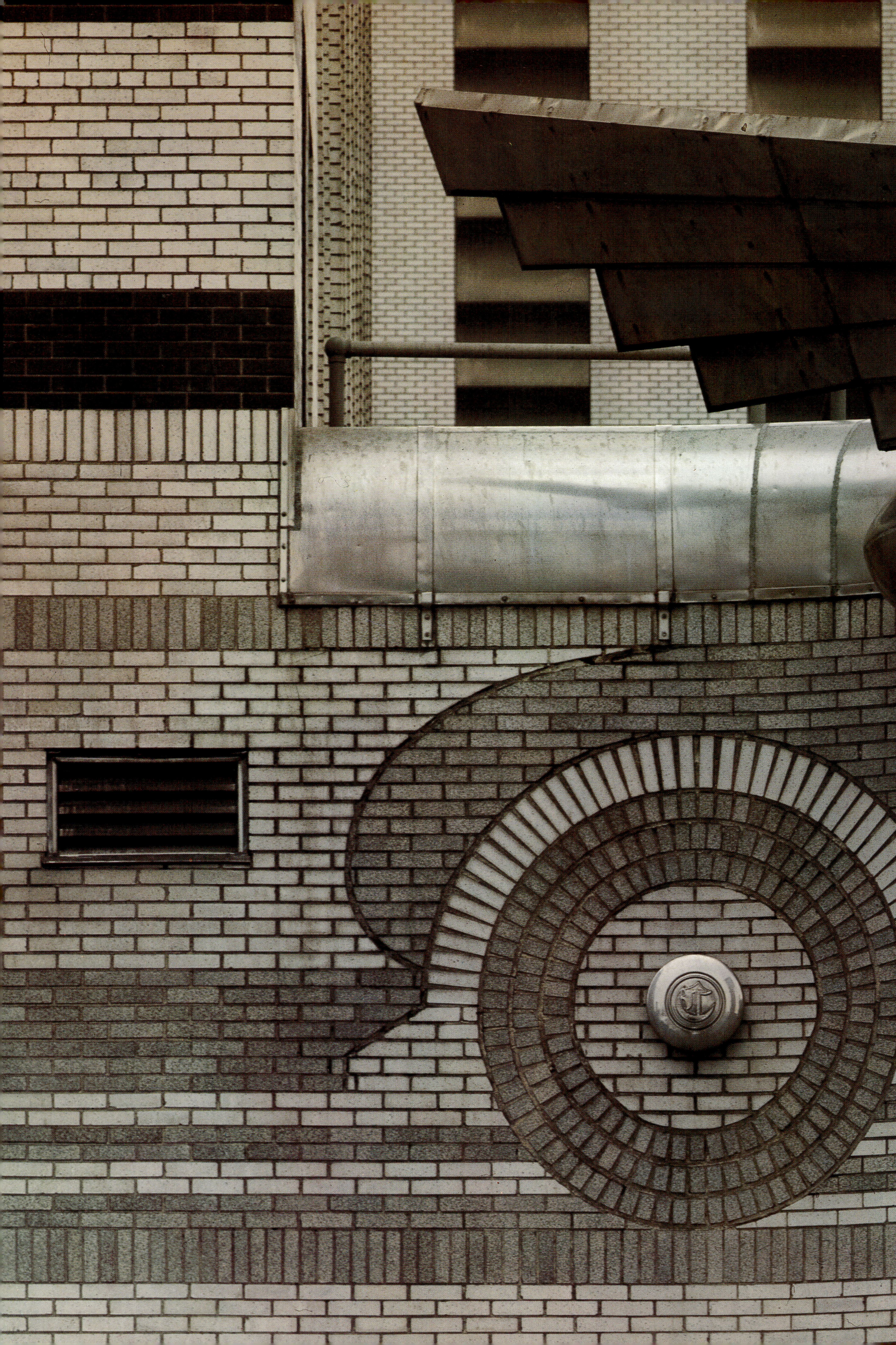

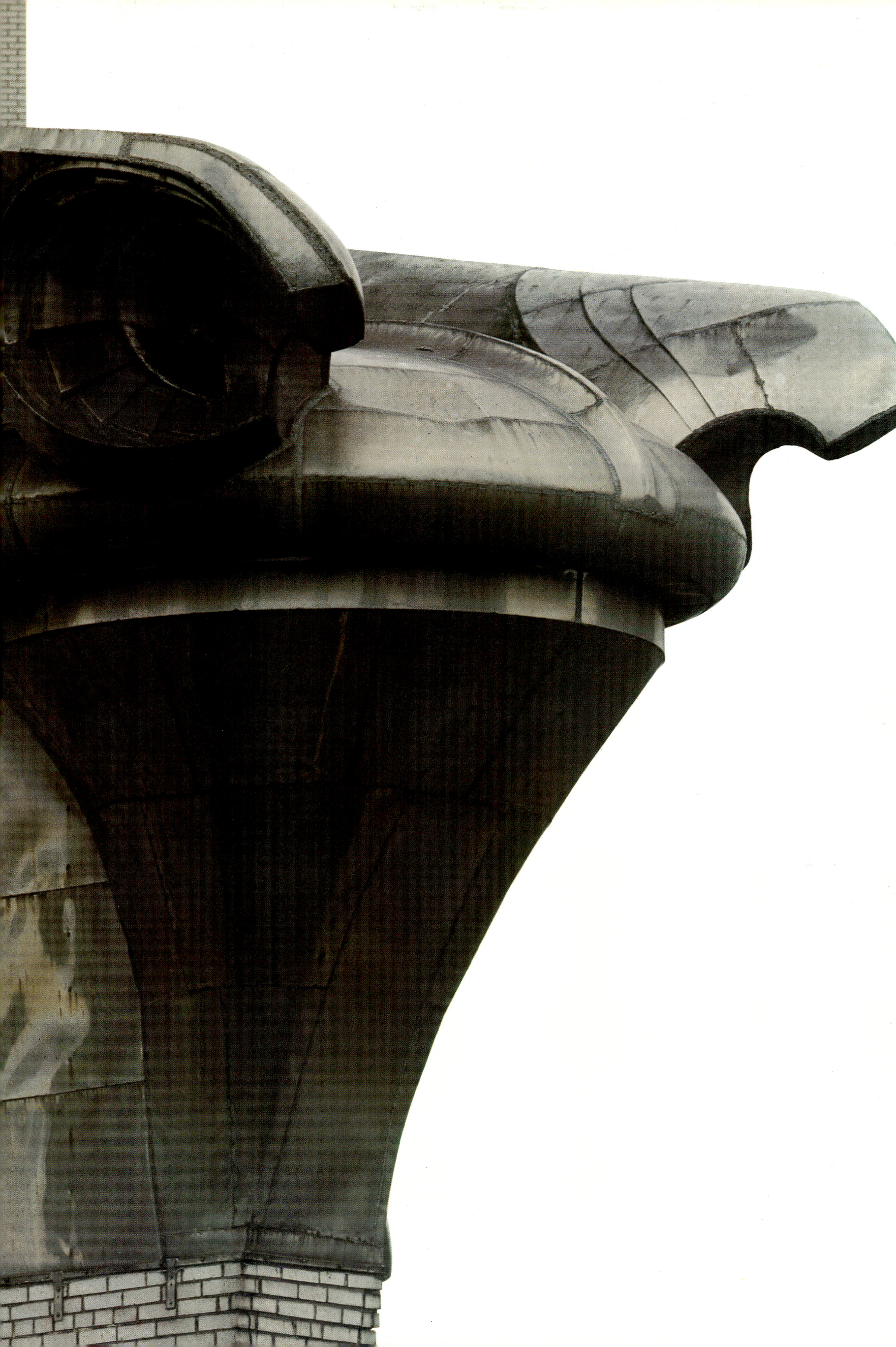

Even those who criticize her are not able to escape New York's dynamic. Returning from Europe to his hometown, Henry James described New York as a monument to transiency, built just for the day – and built expensively. He was nevertheless impressed by the might in those stones.

There is a beauty of light and air, the great scale of space ... But the real appeal, unmistakably, is in that note of vehemence in the local life, for it is the appeal of dauntless power. The aspect the power wears is indescribable; it is the power of the most extravagant of cities, rejoicing, as with the voice of the morning, in its might, its fortune, its unsurpassable conditions, and imparting to every object and element, to the motion and expression of every floating, hurrying, panting thing, to the throb of ferries and tugs, to the splash of waves and the play of winds and the glint of lights and the shrill of whistles and the quality and authority of breeze-born cries – all, practically, a diffused, wasted clamour of detonations – something of its sharp free accent and, above all, of its sovereign sense of being "backed" and able to back.

Henry James

A generation later, Lewis Mumford sang the praises of the majesty of the New York cityscape, which even the most obscene profiteering had not been able to ruin: the dramatic grandeur of the island lying at the mouth of the Hudson and the contrast between the towering stalagmites of its buildings with the rich, Dutch, flat moraine of Long Island. To everyone who tries to describe it, New York presents itself in a new light. For John O'Hara it was "Baghdad on the Subway"; for E. B. White, the world's greatest concentration of humanity; for Damon Runyon, New York was "the Big Apple" – the winning sweepstakes ticket, the jackpot worth the wildest bet. For others, it is a magical vision:

It is a myth, the city, the rooms and windows, the steam-spitting streets; for anyone, everyone, a different myth, an idol-head with traffic-light eyes winking a tender green, a cynical red. This island, floating in river water like a diamond iceberg, call it New York, name it whatever you like; the name hardly matters because, entering from the greater reality of elsewhere, one is only in search of a city, a place to hide, to lose or discover oneself, to make a dream wherein you prove that perhaps after all you are not an ugly duckling, but wonderful, and worthy of love.

Truman Capote

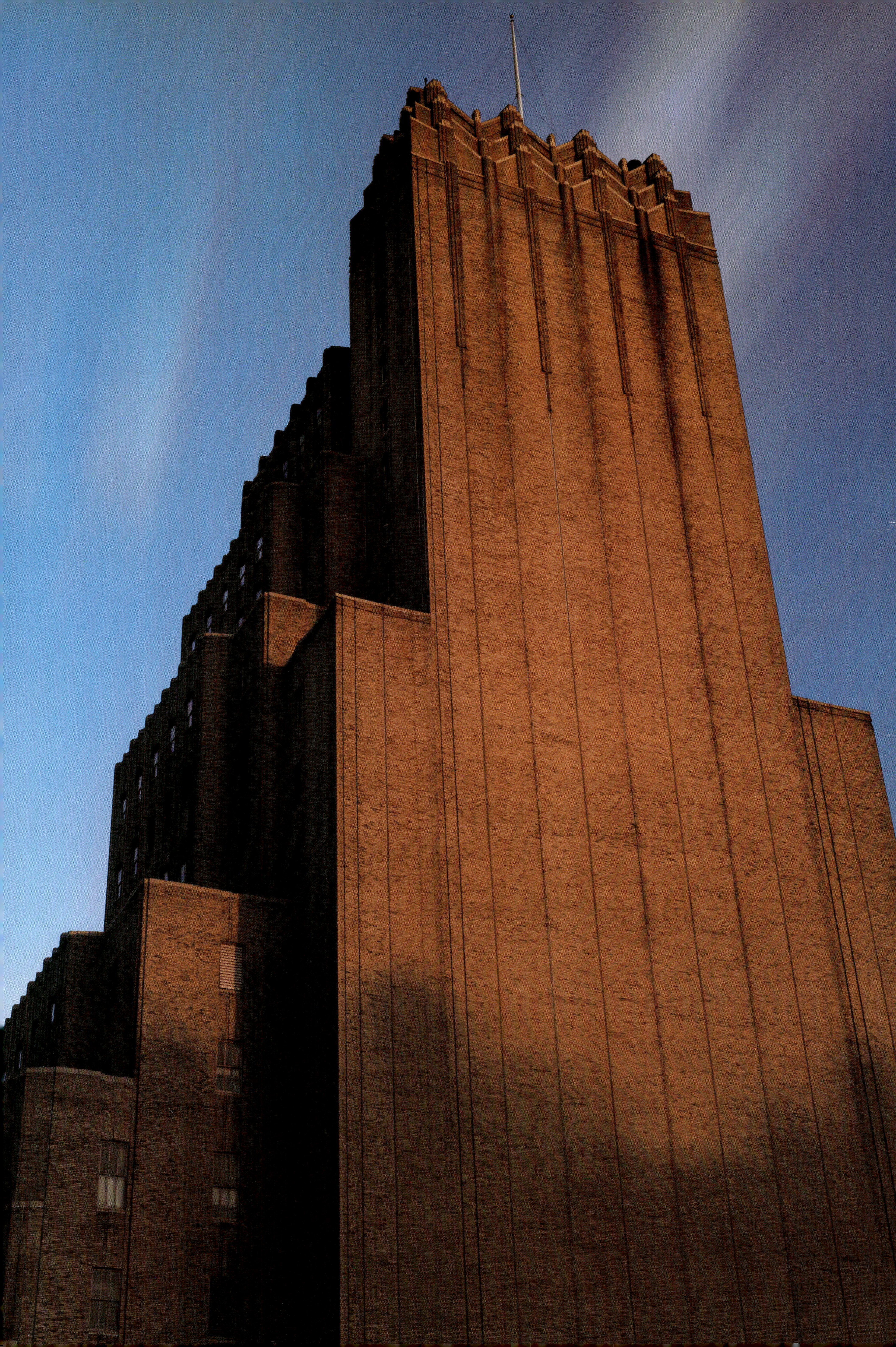

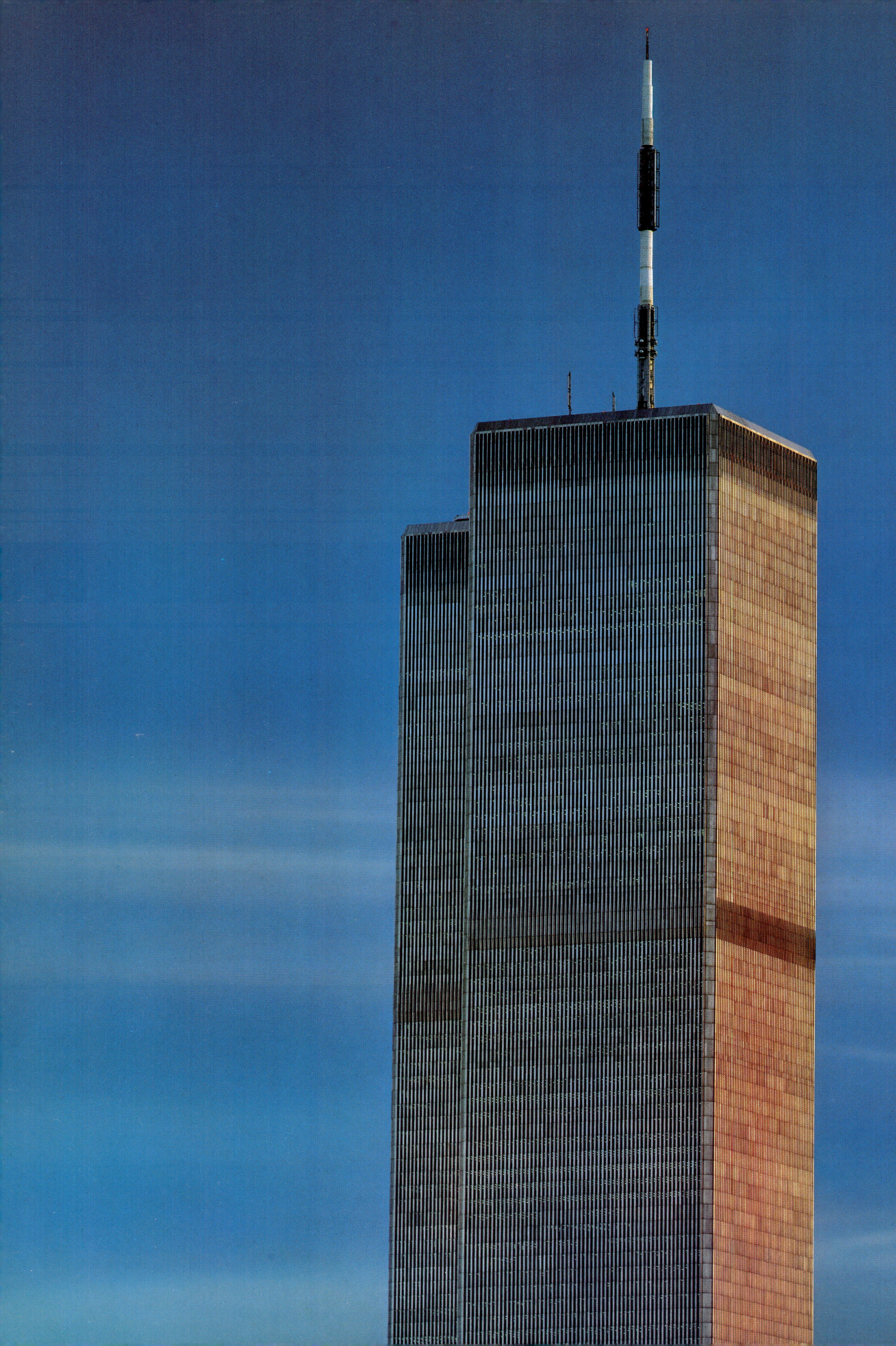

New York is a city of survivors. It is Noah's ark for those
who have fled famine and persecution: fugitives from
tsarist, communist, fascist and religious persecutions, from
the Armenian massacre and from Cuban egalitarianism,
from concentration camps, imprisonment and dispos-
session, from the Irish potato famine and the miseries of
Sicily – escapees one and all. They survived all this and the
rigors and dangers of ocean crossings that took weeks – just
as others survived who came fleeing racial segregation or
the slow death of the intellect in backwood provinces.

They have all become New Yorkers, but the threads
which bind them to their origins have not all been cut. The
"neighborhoods", with their old-country churches, clubs
and cuisine, tell as much of the ethnic diversity and the
almost village-like character of New York as do the polyglot
names of its citizenry. The municipal offices are directed by
people named Impellitteri, Schuldiner, McGillicuddy,
Dziewiontkowski; the hot-dog dealer on the corner is called
Spiridoula Karlamboboulos, and the Manhattan telephone
directory runs from Alec Aaarman to N. Zzherobrouskievs-
kieskieea. All the tribes, races, languages, nations of this
earth have assembled here – and the natives often choose to
stick together, to belong to a "neighborhood". Who would
think that in metropolitan New York there are twenty
thousand Albanians, eight thousand of them Muslims with
their own mosque?

For the interested observer, New York becomes an
ethnic festival, a living museum that preserves the nations
of the world in all their diversity, a great nonstop open-air
theatre of cultural diversity, lending New York its peculiar
charm and vigor.

*I would not want to live anywhere else but in New York.
Here I feel right in the Twentieth Century. No other place,
neither London nor Paris, gives me that feeling of being
"contemporary". If there is anything to compare to this
New York sense of bubbling champagne, it would have
been the Berlin of the Twenties. The same electrifying
atmosphere I experienced in those Berlin years, I find in
New York today; the same confidence that everything that
matters in any department of the arts, is gathered here.*
                                                              Lotte Lenya

The city is not in the habit of dealing gently with its
citizens. This is no place for the thin-skinned. The
gruffness of the New Yorker is proverbial – a product of the
vexations of city life, his way of defending himself against

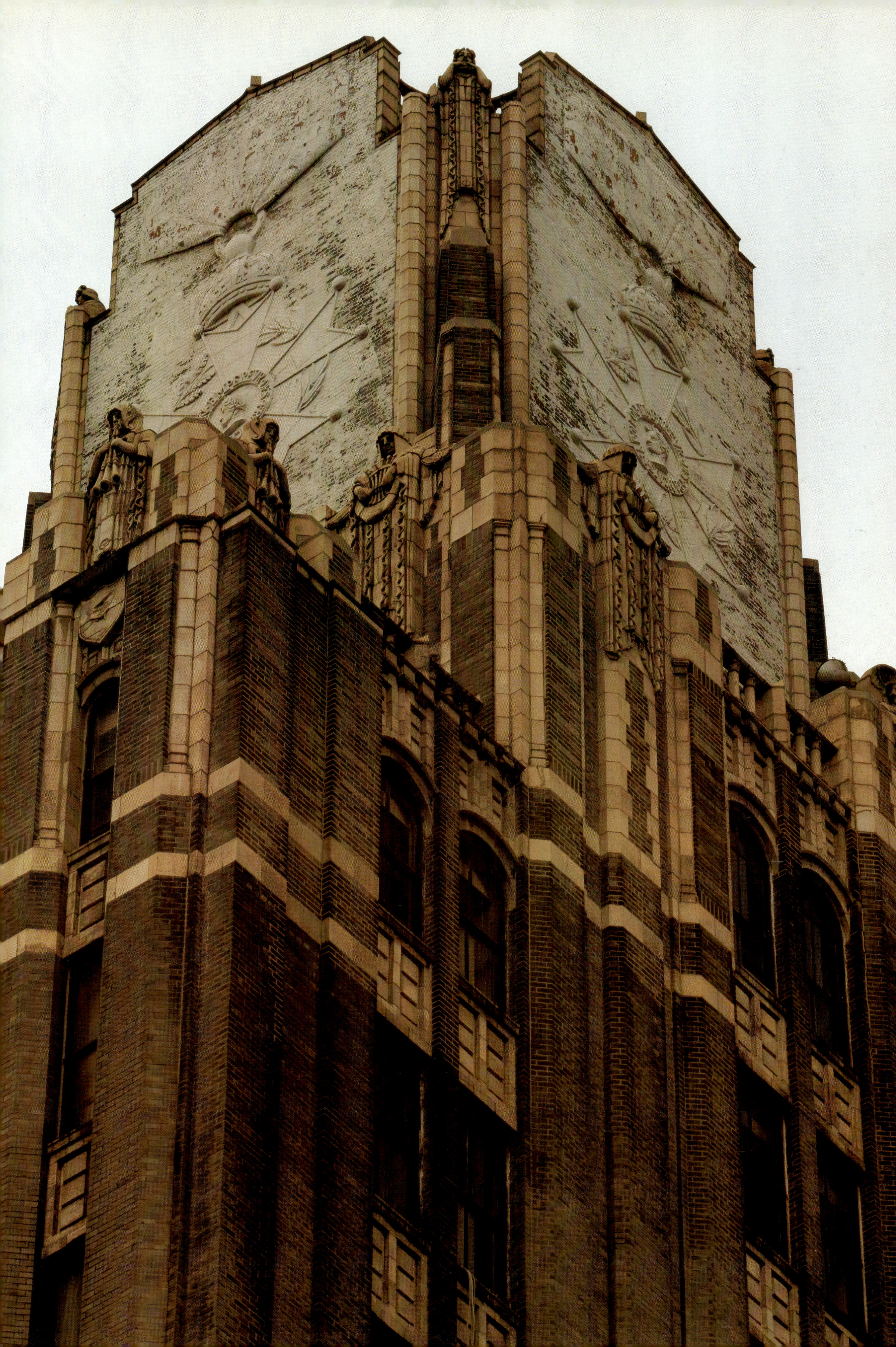

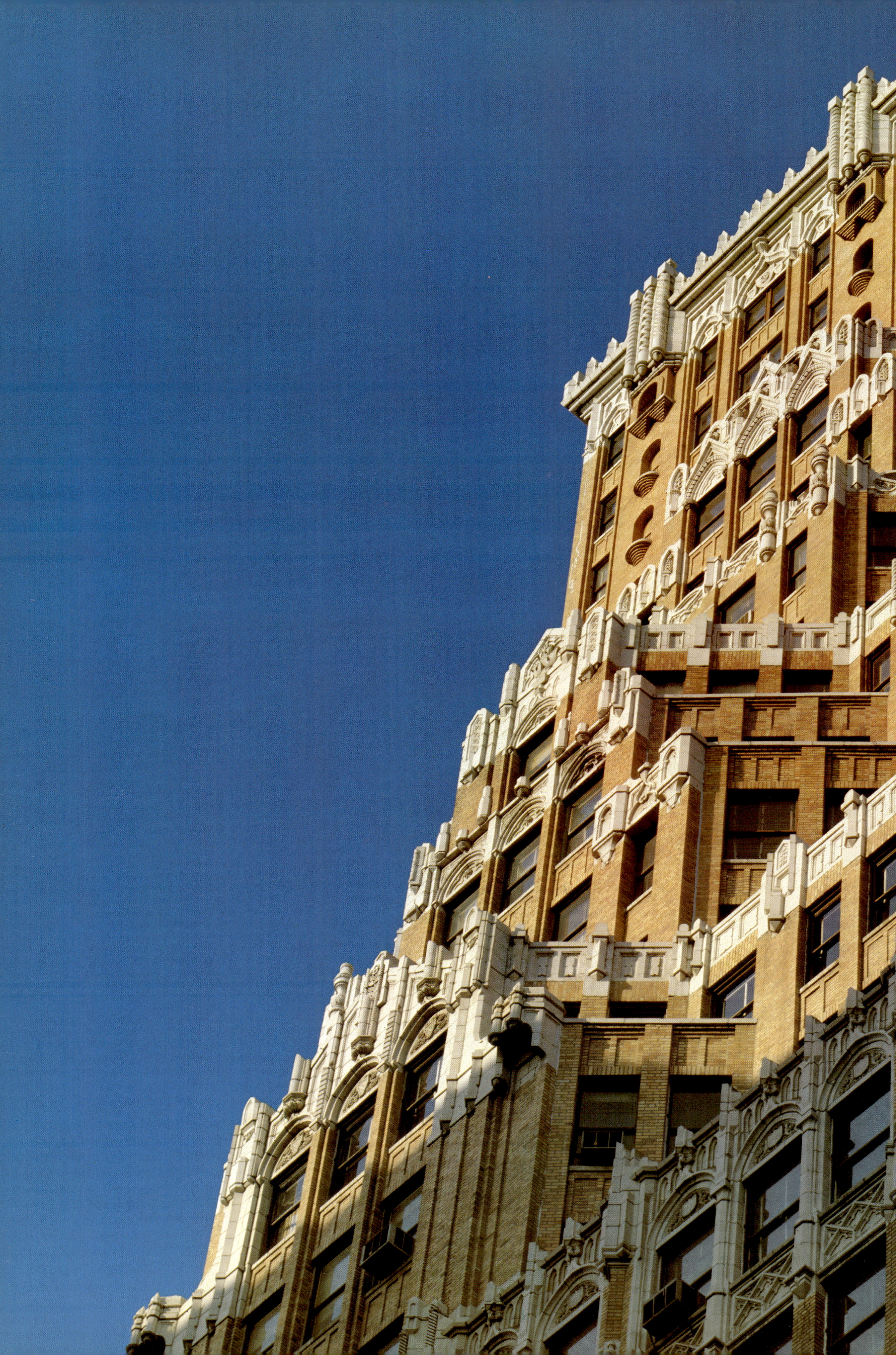

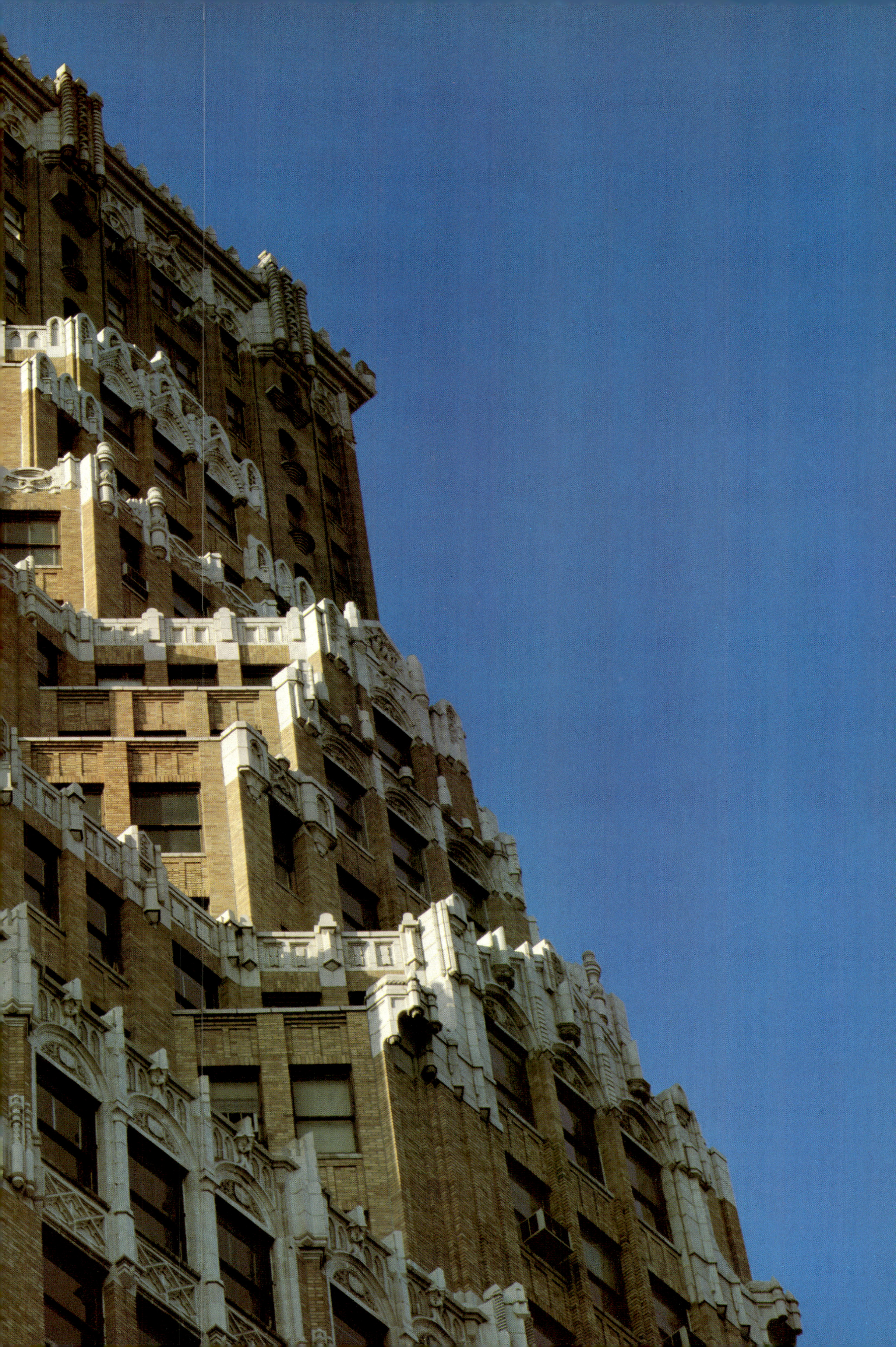

what both the city and nature hurl at him. New York can
seem rude and surly – and it is often brutal. But brutality
isn't necessarily catching, just the opposite: the daily
struggle with harsh reality elicits a countervailing mildness
from many New Yorkers. Where yesterday the city seemed
possessed by a rage for self-destruction and its inhabitants
had apparently sworn to make life as difficult as possible
for one another, today it seems a heaven for the world's
Good Samaritans, each trying to outdo the other in works of
mercy. Brutality and benevolence, swindlers and
samaritans, rich and poor, cosmopolitans and provincials
live here elbow to elbow. New York is a city of contradic-
tions and extremes. Everything that happens here is
somehow more visible than elsewhere, the very contrasts
give it all a harder edge. In New York a poor man is poorer
still. The wares of the marketplace are piled high around
him; the vast array of goods and hopes set expectations
rising – and the lack of means hurts just that much more.
Incomparable luxury and the most miserable slums both
share a Fifth Avenue address.

Our streets are without a doubt the dirtiest in the world.
Garbage is heaped up, the gutters are filled, and yet foreigners
keep coming and coming and coming, searching as if in a
foreign market for something they cannot find at home. One
day as I was coming out of a restaurant on Madison Avenue
with a French friend, a stiff breeze swept up the avenue
and this charming French fellow and I were covered with
cigarette butts, scraps of dirty newspaper and everything
that exists in our streets. I turned and said: "What do you
come here for when you live in such a beautiful, clean
environment at home?" and he answered: "You Americans
do not understand. New York is great. Few regulations are
kept here, faces are different, every language is spoken –
it is like an ancient oriental city and it excites all of us. We
love it." I replied: "I love it, too."

Diana Vreeland

Through this sea of paradoxes the New Yorker
navigates. His life has all the tension of a balancing act in
the circus. The city will let you be a hermit, if you wish, but
it will never let you be alone. You may pursue your intel-
lectual pleasures, but the city offers no ivory tower among
its skyscrapers. Danger is compensated for by delight, bad
manners by an act of kindness, a cussing-out from a truck
driver by a "honey" or a "darling" from your waitress at the
coffee-counter. The art is to take it all in like a sponge – and
let no one squeeze you dry.

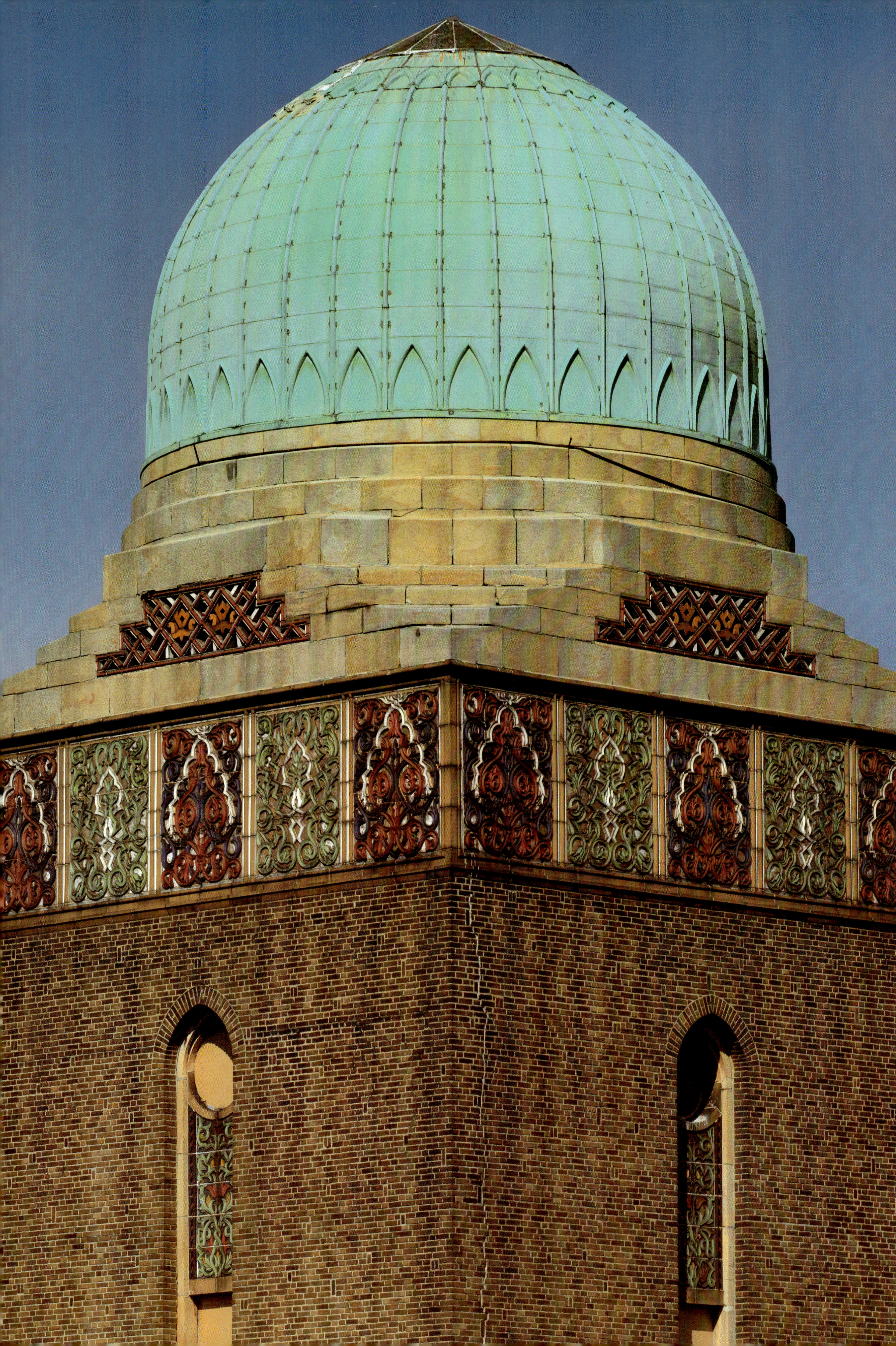

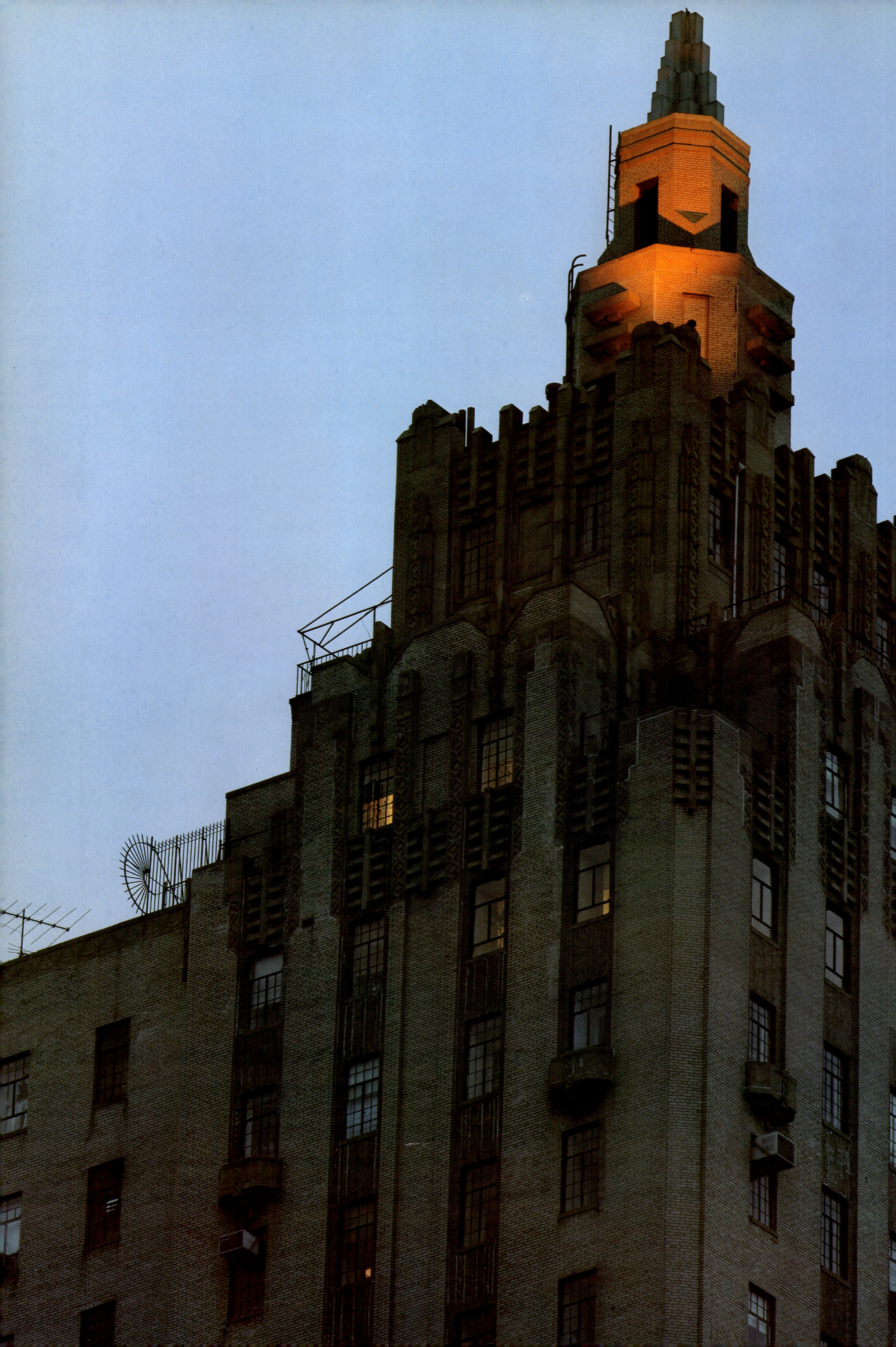

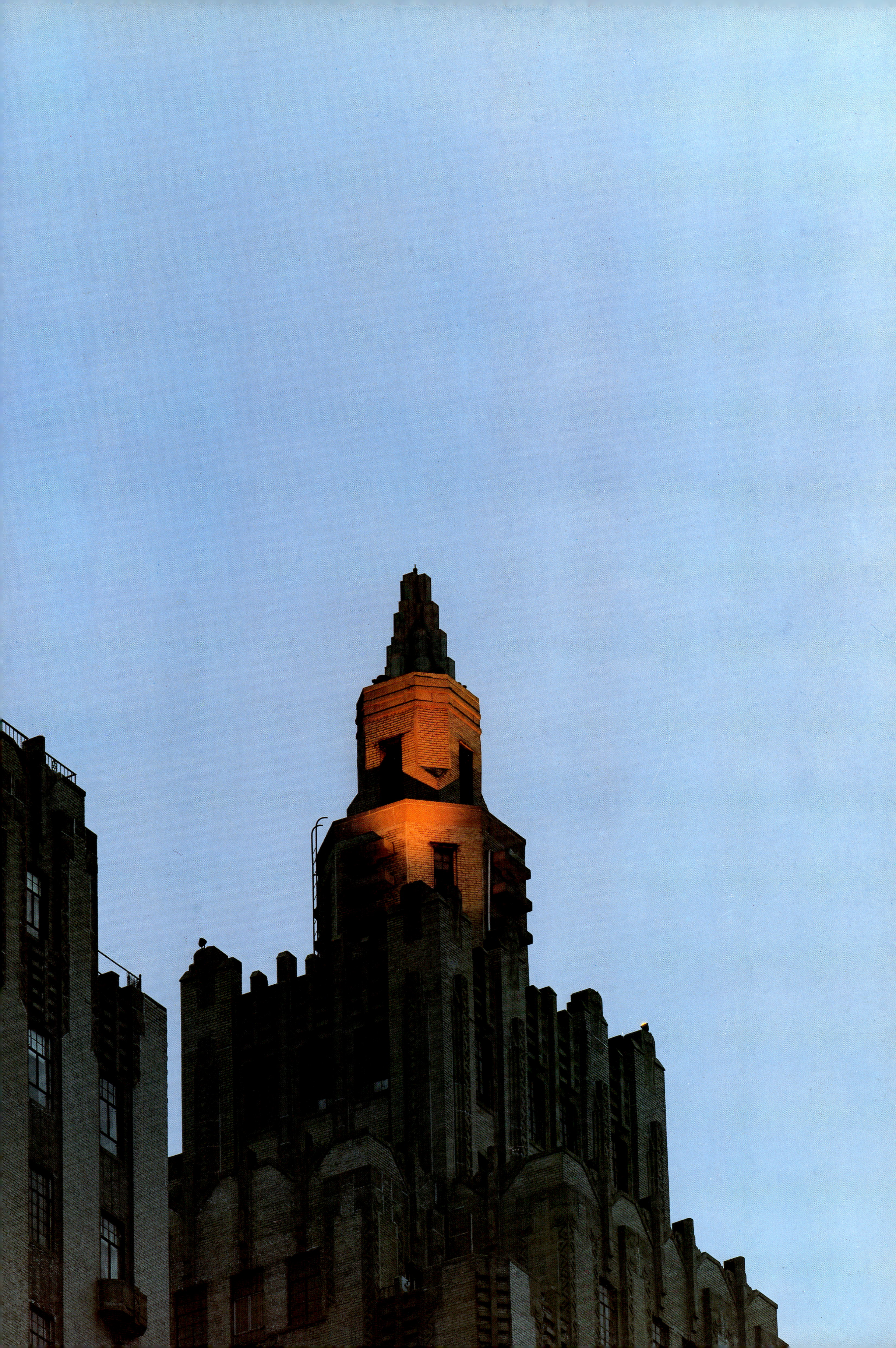

The betting is high, but so is the jackpot. The real New Yorker loves to play this urban roulette, where the wheel starts a new spin with each new day.

The young woman executive balancing the double role of mother and careerwoman uses the city to her advantage in a twofold way. She accepts the challenges and the possibilities the city has to offer, building her business by the law of supply and demand. At the same time, she expects the city to serve as school and university for her children whom she does not send to boarding-school. She wants rather for them to grow up in New York because she would like to see them "use" the city and grow with it and in it. Life in New York, this mother thinks, is a full and complete education.

In New York, as in physics, every action has its reaction. Where speculation in real estate becomes as ruthless as the profits are immense, there too idealists band together to do sentimental battle for every old house, for every brick wall on the block. Remnants of façades that have been razed – the bases of columns, bits of pediment, caryatids – are saved from the hammer's blow and placed in their own hall of honor in the Brooklyn Museum. Having to live with cockroaches and rats only paves the way for an even more determined love of nature. There are a dozen birdwatcher clubs in the city, and their weatherproof members who roam the parks, binoculars in hand, know all four hundred species of bird that nest here or merely stop for a visit. Even the New York sunsets are a gift of chemical pollution. The fumes and vapors which New Jersey sends the city's way, raining soot and grime, filter out the blues of twilight and put the sun to rest beyond the palisades of the Hudson in a burst of brilliant reds and oranges, bathing Manhattan in alpenglow.

The people who live in this city feel challenged by it, and if the city doesn't defeat you, then you grow right along with it. Granted, you have to be willing to work with the city, not against it. If it is true that cities reflect the moods and energy of their inhabitants and visitors – seem grim to the sullen soul and yet warmly open-armed to the glad of heart – then it is that much more true of New York. This city pays back just what you invest in it. New York works like a watershed. There are those who feel themselves exalted, enriched, animated, who feel their energies and their love of life expand. And there are those whom the city frightens, depresses, whose reaction is one of claustrophobia and repulsion.

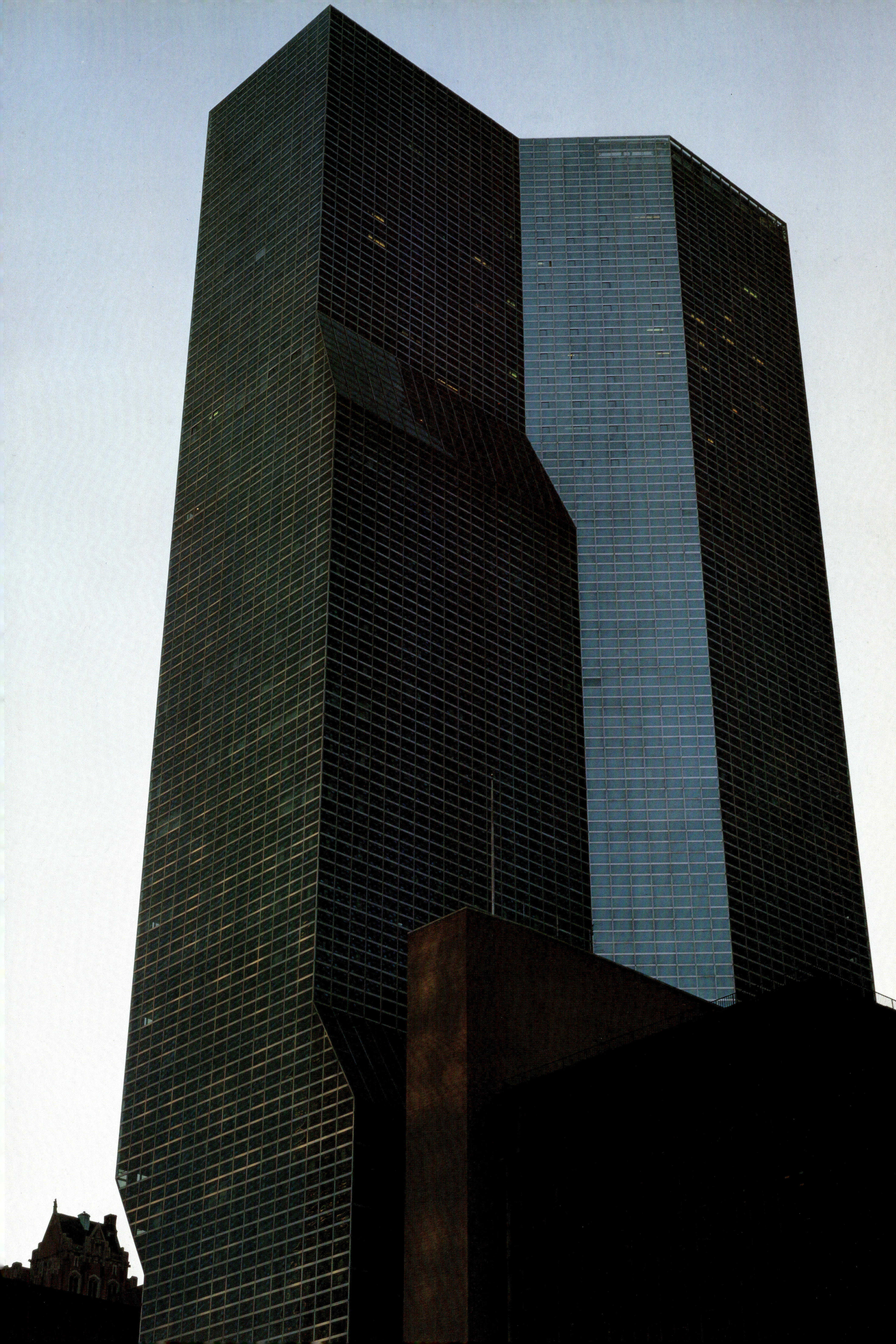

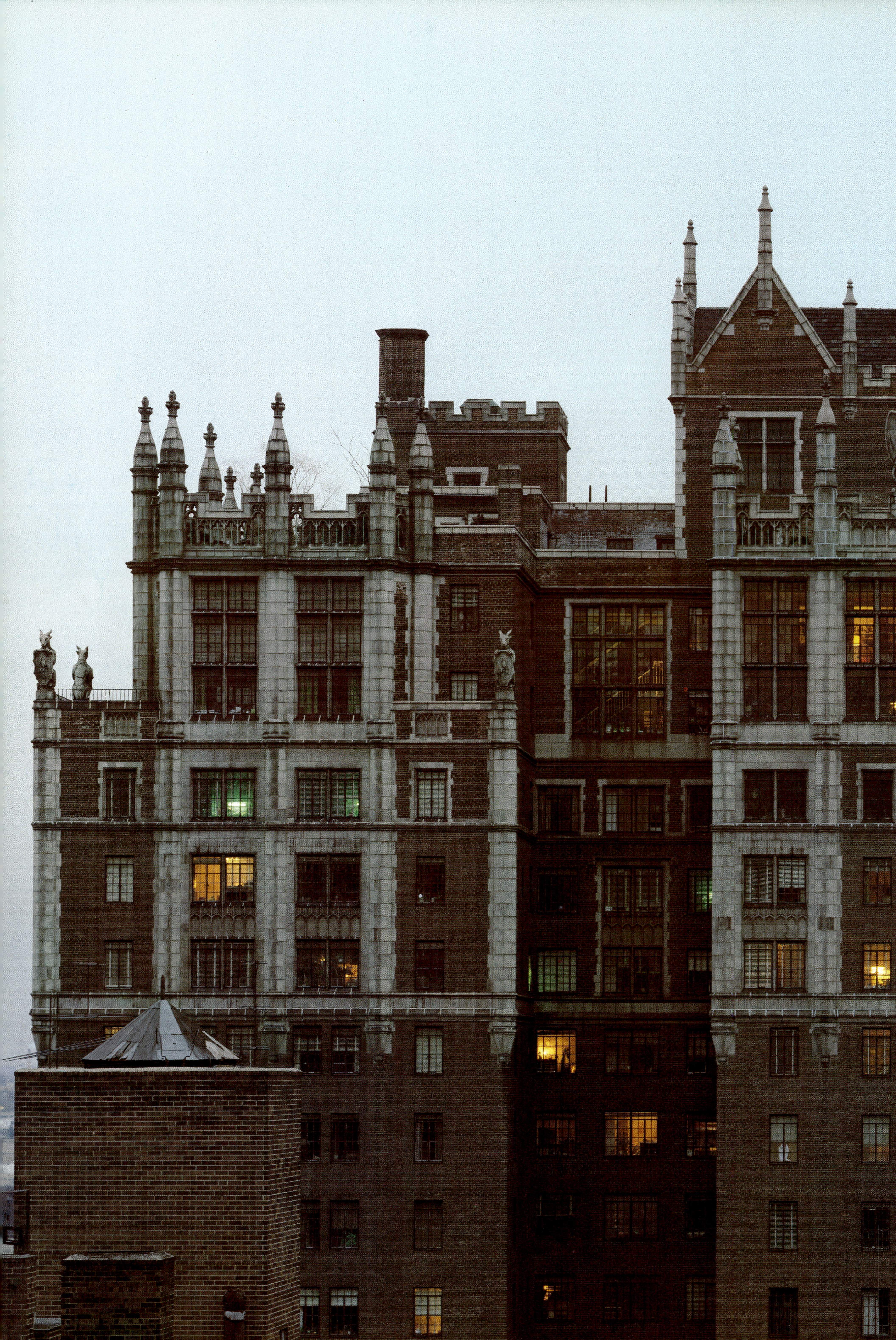

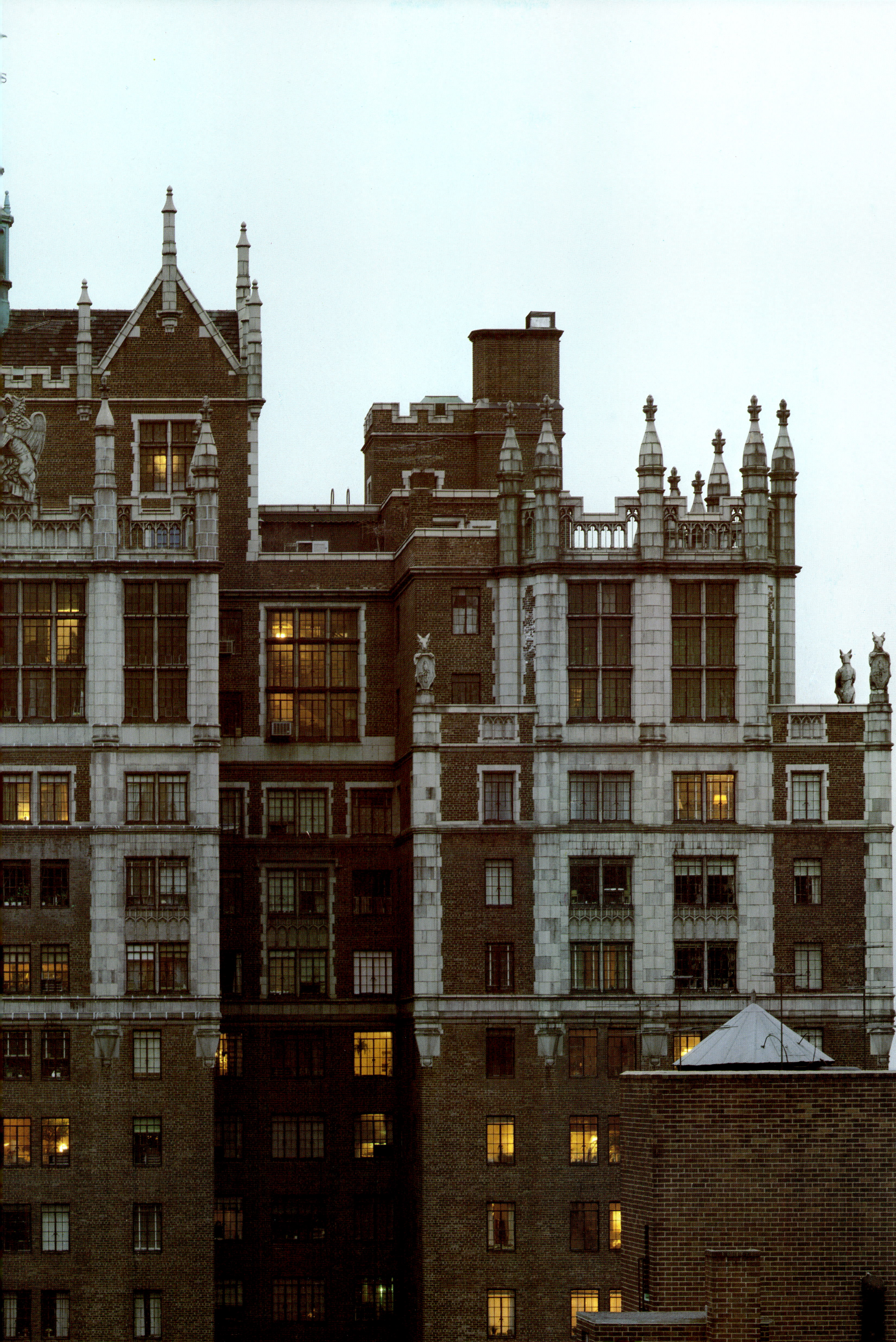

To live here is to experience how much a city can mirror life's moods. The streets are dismal for anyone who takes to them feeling disgruntled.

But it takes only a few ounces of curiosity and tolerance, a dash of love for adventure and new experiences, and New York will generously oblige the kindly disposed observer. The doormen in their uniforms from some silly operetta, the splashing of the fountains in the apartment-house lobbies – yesterday they seemed gaudy and foolish, today there is something cheery and playful about them. Everyone you meet is in a good mood, and those endless rows of buildings with their fire escapes and crowning watertanks are no longer horrors, but something special and typically "New York". Out of curiosity you make inquiries and discover that those round, wooden structures up on the roofs are the work of a certain Mr. Rosenwach, whose grandfather manufactured barrels for sauerkraut and pickles. You notice the quaint and personal side of the city: the branch office of a bank where a lady plays the piano every Wednesday; Raymond the Bagel-Man with his pushcart – City College awarded him the academic degree of "Bachelor of Pretzel Purveyance" for 25 years of faithful service; a decorative group of columns, saved from some demolished building, which now stand in front of the ultramodern Police Headquarters; the little vegetable garden, complete with scarecrow, on Third Avenue. You need to take in New York with all five senses: the green-grocers with their dangling scales and the street lamps shaped like bishops' crosiers, the aroma of roasting chest-nuts in winter and the smell of the ocean in summer, screeching gulls and the moan of foghorns, the staccato of the New York dialect and the warm intimacy of a drugstore counter with its unmistakable smell blending perfume with bacon frying. The open-eyed and open-minded observer feels how the city inspires and energizes him, how it forms and reforms itself as a continuous adventure, a promise without end.

Hideously ugly for the most part, one yet remembers it as a place of proud and passionate beauty; the place of everlasting hunger, it is also the place where men feel their lives will gloriously be fulfilled and their hunger fed … There is no place like it, no place with an atom of its glory, pride and exultancy. It lays its hand upon a man's bowels; he grows drunk with ecstasy; he grows young and full of glory, he feels that he can never die.

Thomas Wolfe

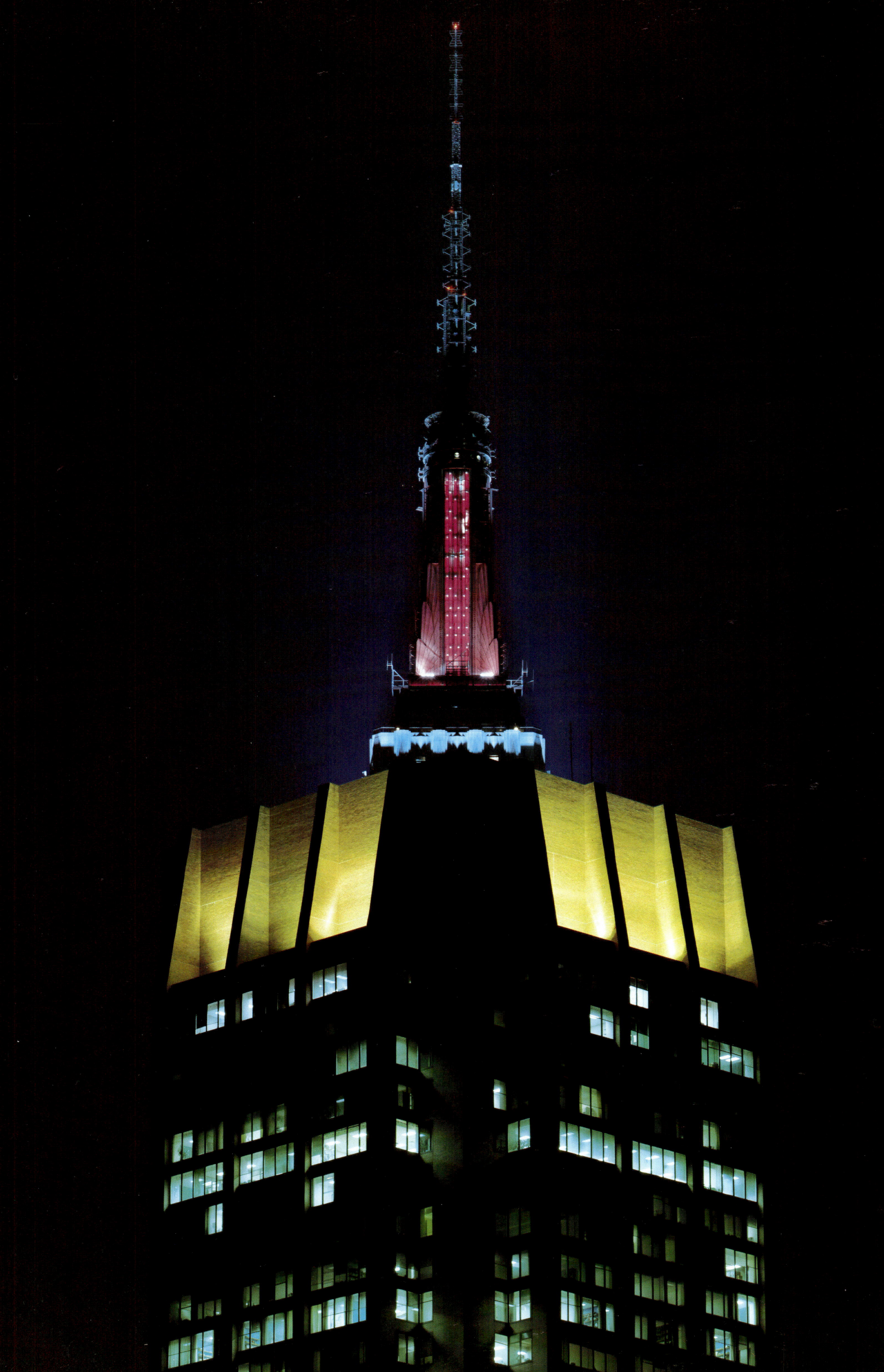

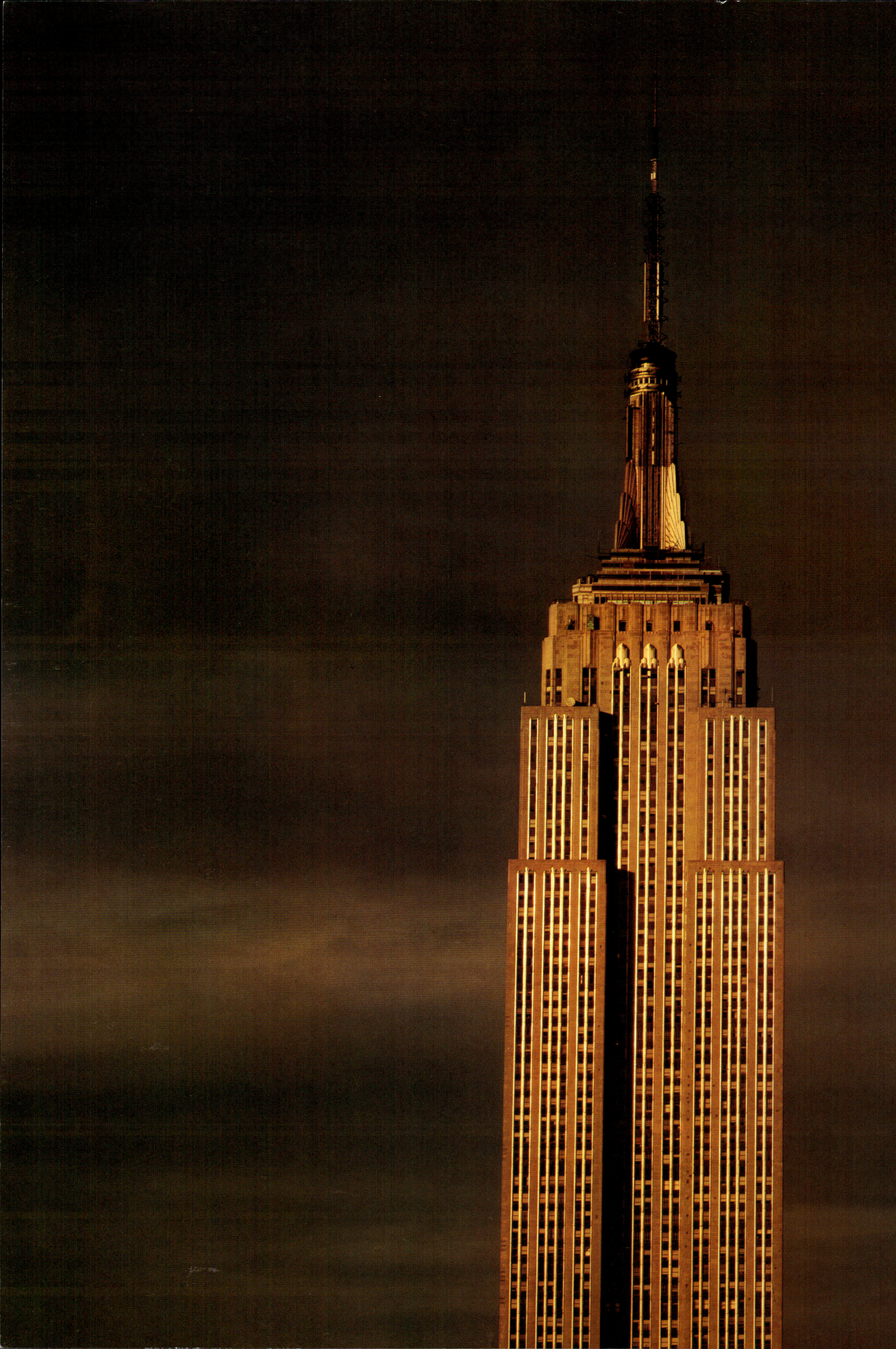

Thomas Wolfe wrote that in the 1930's in his autobiographical novel "The Web and the Rock", but that zest for life which he describes is something the city offers to each new generation that is ready to be tested, eager to be challenged by it. For the historian of our own times, New York is just as much "my city" as it was for the poet of the last century.

That bold, brilliant, crafty, luminous, ominous city, so streaked with light and shadow, so rich in achievement and possibility, so sinister at midnight, so lovely at dawn. At once the most American and the most international of cities, every language heard on its street, a city of the past and of the future, overflowing with vitality and menace, New York endures in pride, ambiguity, promise. The city's greatest poet, Walt Whitman, said it all one hundred and twenty years ago in "Mannahatta":
... A word, liquid, sane, unruly, musical, self-sufficient ...
... An island sixteen miles long, solid-founded,
Numberless crowded streets, high growths of iron, slender,
*   strong, light, splendidly uprising toward clear skies ...*
A million people – manners free and superb – open voices –
*   hospitality – the most courageous and friendly*
*   young men,*
City of hurried and sparkling waters!
City of spires and masts!
City nested in bays! My city!   *Arthur Schlesinger, jr.*

New York gets its hooks into your memory: those intense colors of dusk when the nearness of the sea turns the towers gold; the sparkling light of the thousands upon thousands of electric stars scattered across the city by night; the bridges with their gestures of elegance; the unexpected broad vistas of the Manhattan landscape. The sky turns a golden red out over an ocean that sends a breeze and gulls to visit the city, while in the distance midtown's ridges jut skywards and the lights go up behind the glass walls of the office buildings. You walk across the Brooklyn Bridge, the inspiration of poets and painters, and before you lies the panorama of Manhattan – that has lived on to fulfill in a special way Walt Whitman's vision dating back to the era of sailing vessels: "Stand up, tall masts of Mannahatta!" The bridge itself is a miracle of stone pylons and webs of steel cable. In 1883 when it was opened to traffic it was a triumph of the engineer's art, as admired and celebrated as the Suez Canal to which it was compared. Of all New York's bridges, the Brooklyn Bridge is the trademark of New York

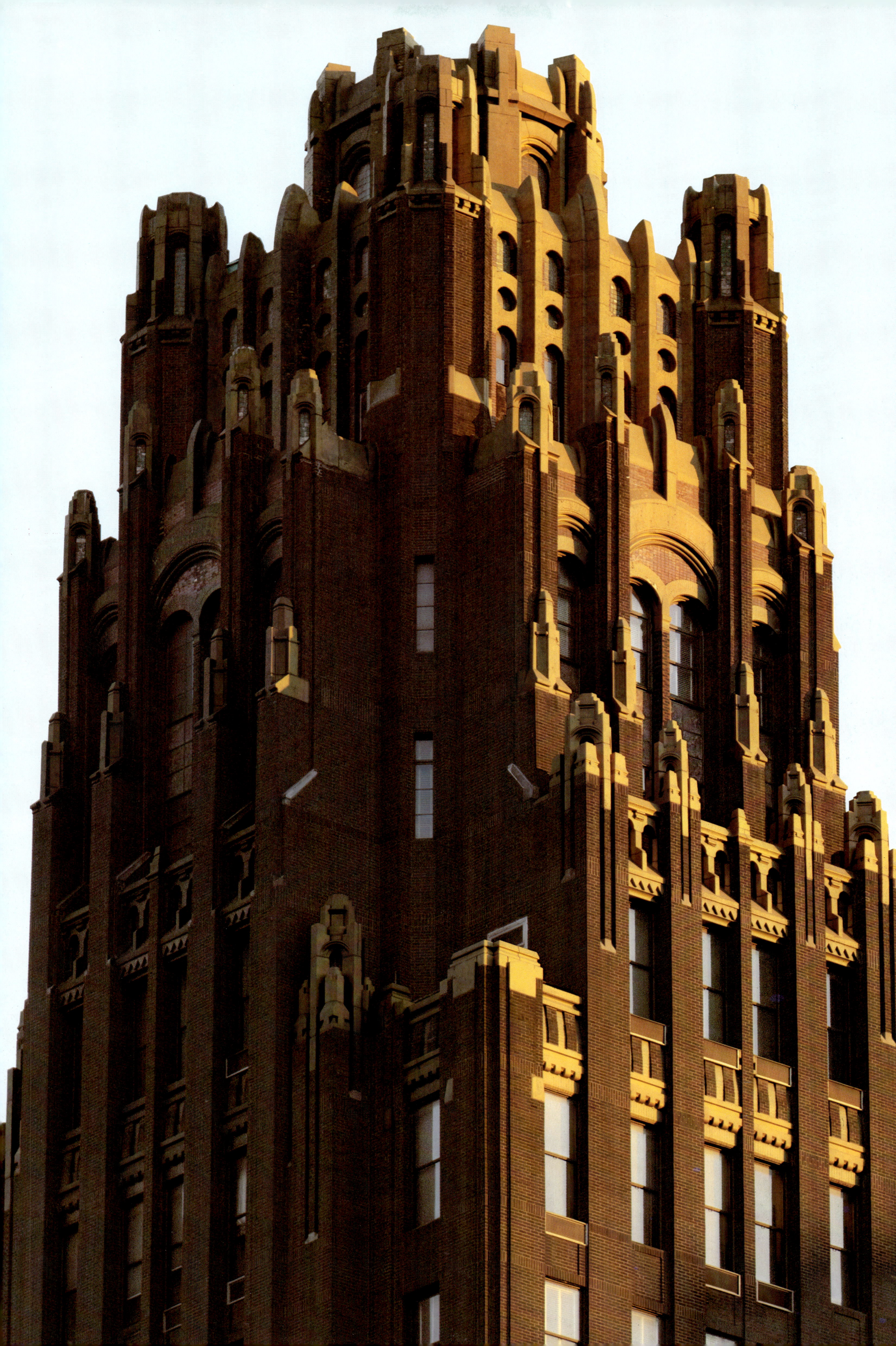

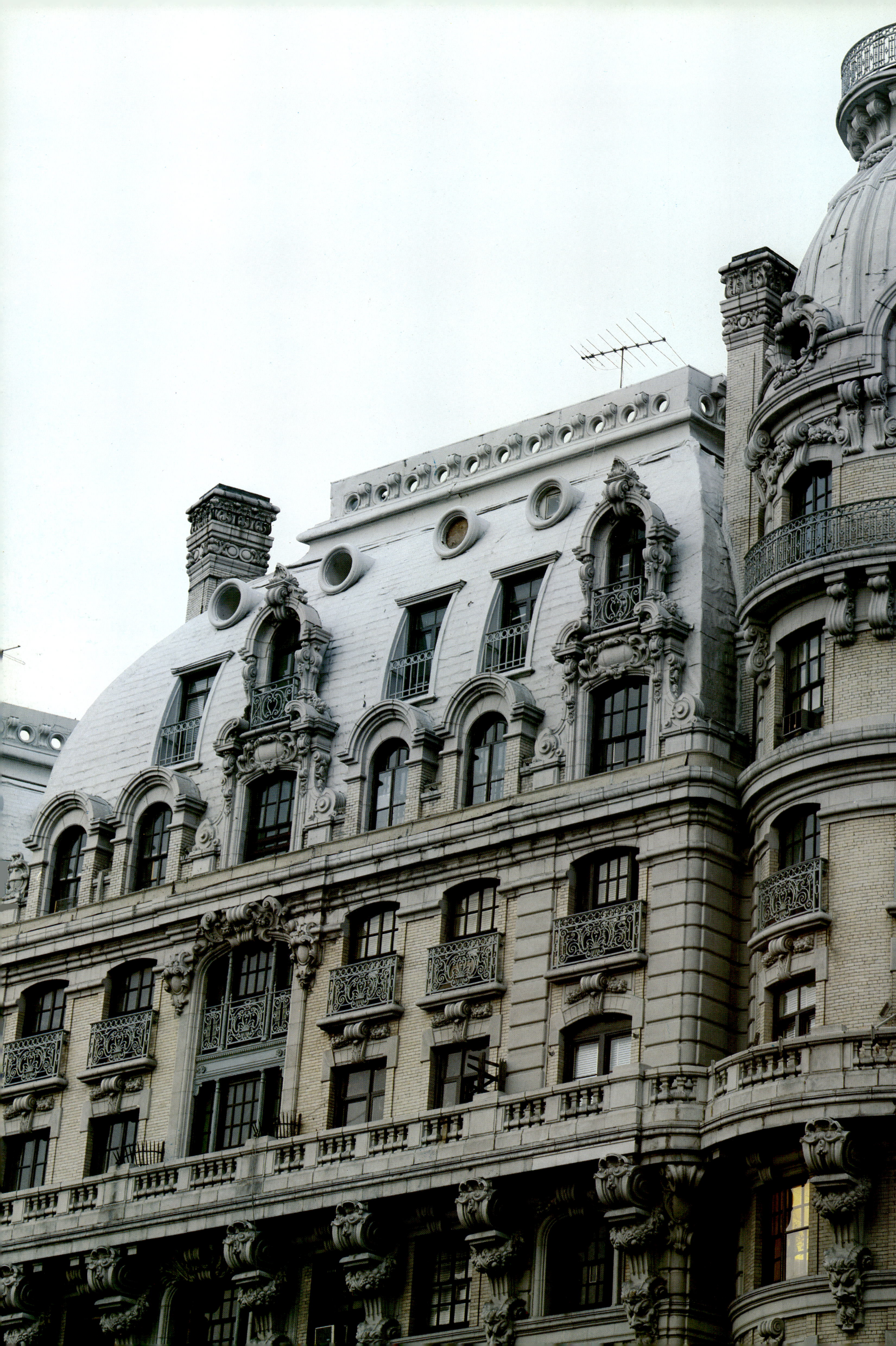

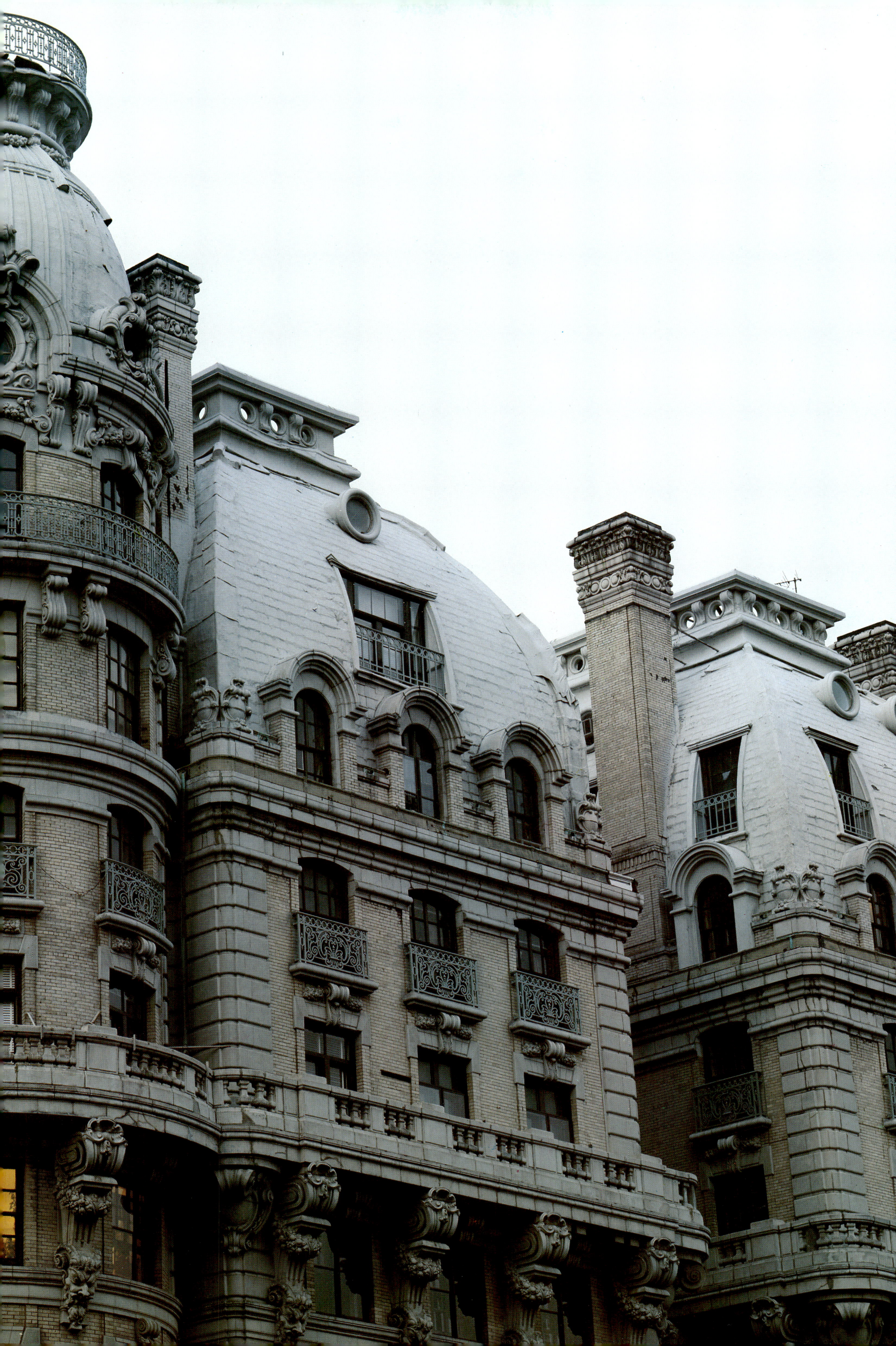

and, at least in Hart Crane's verse, the mythical symbol of
America:

> *... O harp and altar, of the fury fused,*
> *(How could mere toil align thy choiring strings!)*
> *Terrific threshold of the prophet's pledge,*
> *Prayer of pariah, and the lover's cry, – ...*

Functional and fantastic, solid and elegant, a phantom come
home to rest – the Brooklyn Bridge is the entryway to that
city great and high.

At the tip of the island lies the city's financial district,
Manhattan's monument to itself, erected not by plan but by
the accidents of history. The gains and losses, the glory and
the violence, the sum of all the traits in the character of
New York are piled high in a towering drama. There is
dignity and there is vulgarity here, there is muscle-popping
brutality and the elegiac gesture, an unquenchable thirst for
profits next to open-handed generosity. History is here, but
so too is its frenzied disavowal; stone runs amok, only
suddenly to hesitate and stop short. And always there is
change. This is New York in a nutshell, in a snapshot, its
motion frozen for one moment, but the details will be very
different within a year – no, within a week. New spikes
will have been thrust skyward, new glass palaces will be
mirrored in the rivers. What remains is the indestructible
dynamic that survives all change.

It is this scene which poets have described with enthu-
siasm and alarm. It is Walt Whitman's "city of spires and
masts". These are the skyscrapers that Henry James saw
sticking out "like extravagant pins in a cushion already
overplanted", whose "enchanting music as they struggle for
power" the painter John Marin came to hear – clarion
calls of a haughty arrogance.

Here the skyscraper is not an element in city planning,
but a banner in the sky, a fireworks-rocket, an aigrette in
the coiffure of a name henceforth listed in the financial
Almanach de Gotha. Beneath the immaculate office on the
fifty-sixth floor, the vast nocturnal festival of New York
spreads out. No one can imagine it who has not seen it. It is
a titanic mineral display, a prismatic stratification shot
through with an infinite number of lights from top to
bottom, in depth, in a violent silhouette like a fever chart
beside a sickbed. A diamond, incalculable diamonds ...
New York standing up above Manhattan is like a rose-
colored stone in the blue of a maritime sky; New York at
night is like a limitless cluster of jewels.   *Le Corbusier*

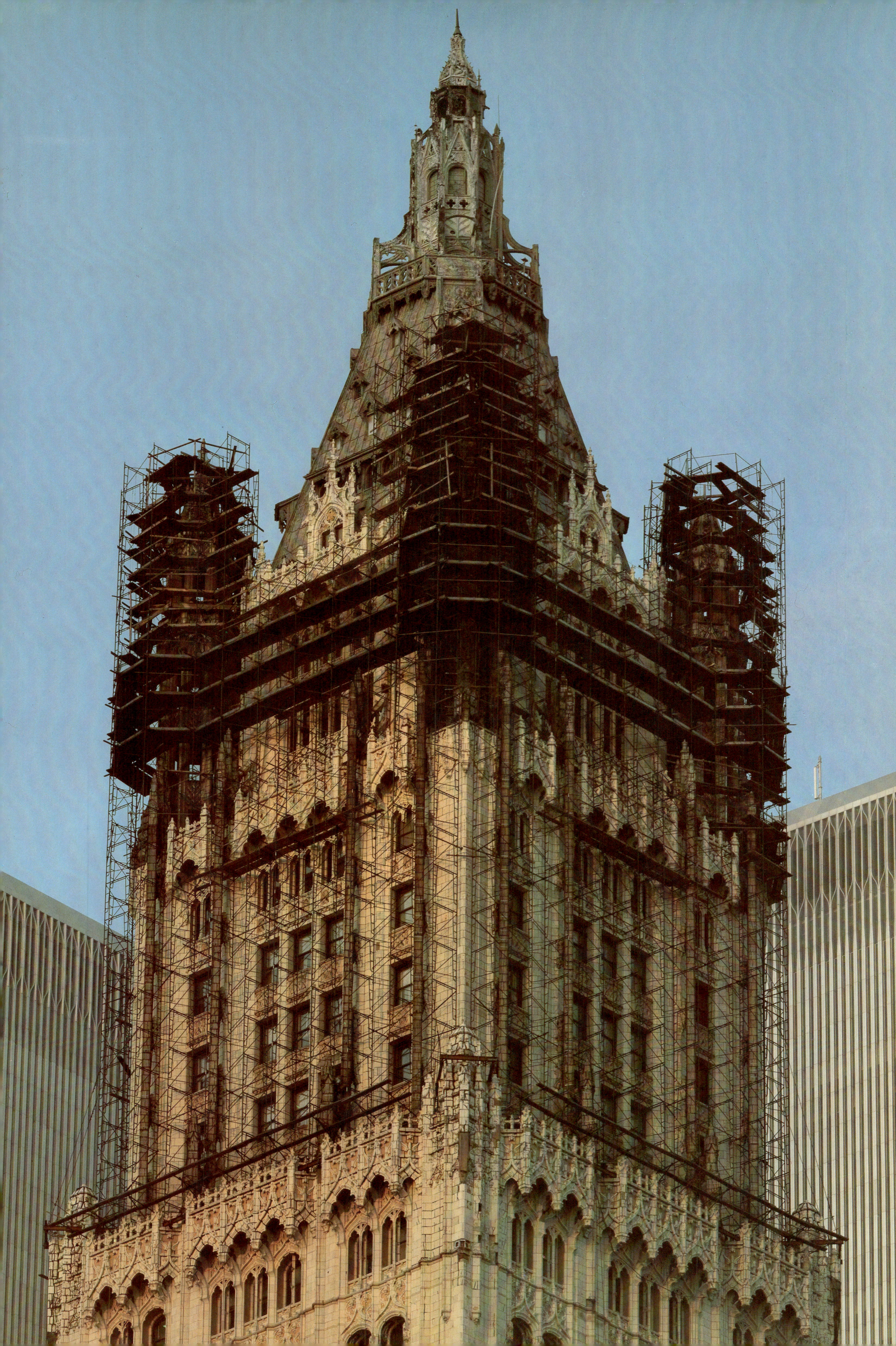

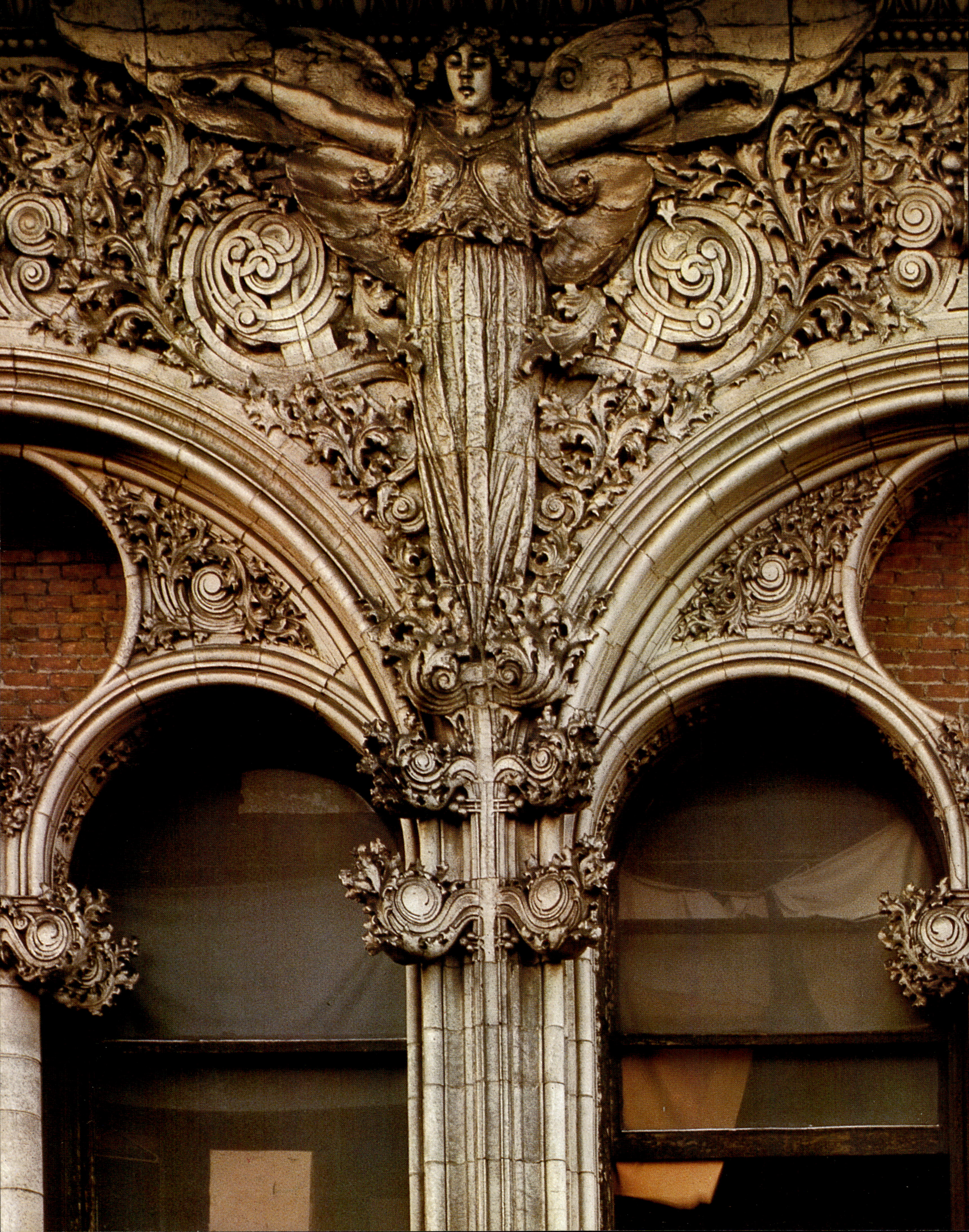

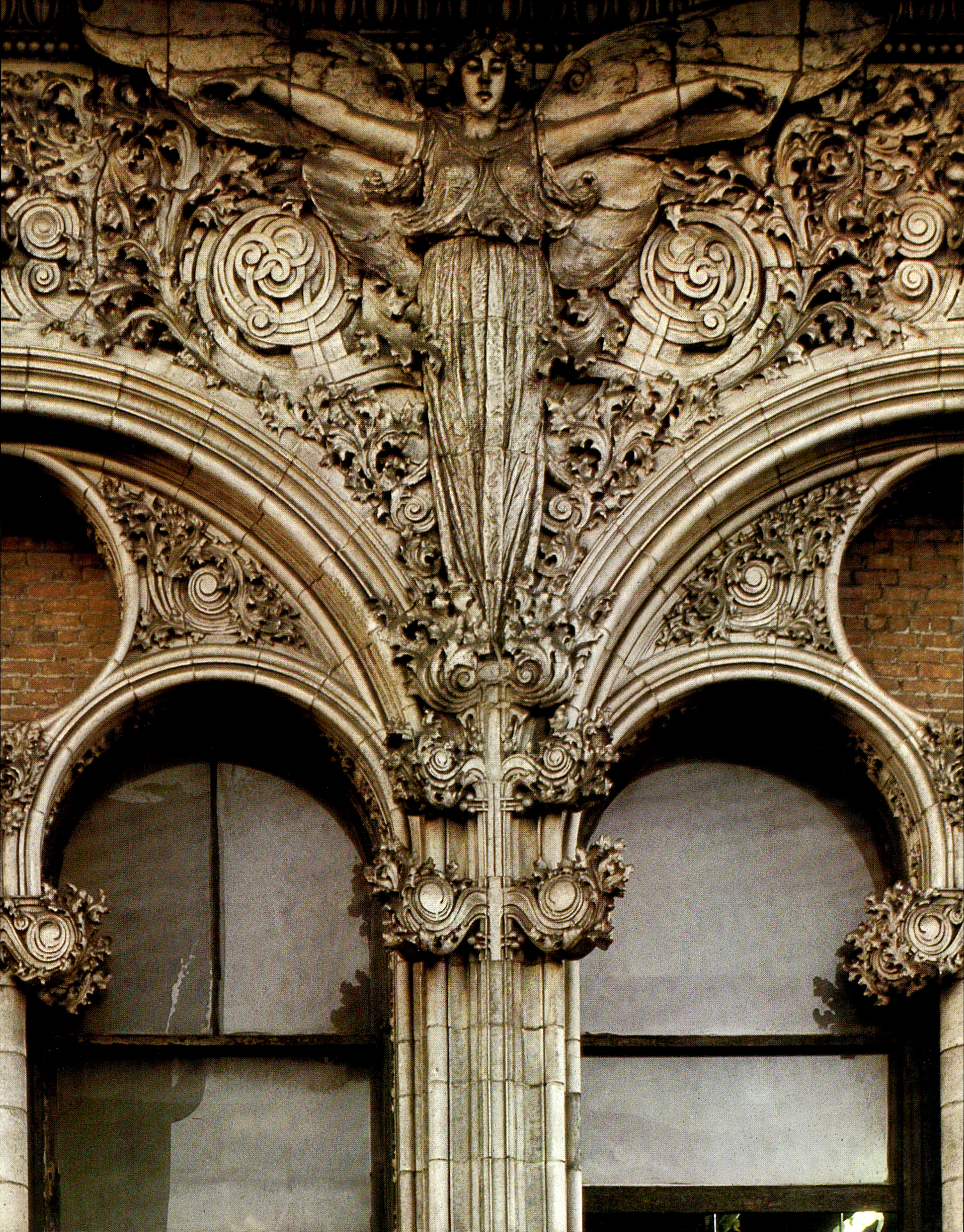

You must learn how to see all over again in New York. The traditional European categories are of little use here. Buildings in New York often take their beauty from their effect, from the way they catch the eye along the sweep of an avenue, from some accent of detail, from disruption of the endless gridiron pattern of the streets. The prow of the Flatiron Building plows its way up Broadway like an ocean liner. The intersection of Sixth Avenue and Tenth Street is embossed with the red bricks of a medieval castle, the Jefferson Market Courthouse. Above the broad promenades of Park Avenue stands the turret of the Pan Am Building, the textured screen of its façade serving as a backdrop to the helmet atop Grand Central Station. From the streets of the West Village you can see the masts of the ships docked along the Hudson, and the view westwards from most any point in midtown provides a glimpse of the New Jersey palisades on the horizon. New York is a city of vistas, of distances; the aesthetic values, proper for European capitals, do not do it justice.

My European, my myopic glance, advancing slowly and prying into everything, tried in vain to find something in New York to arrest it – anything, no matter what – a row of houses suddenly barring the way, the turning of a street, some house weathered and tanned by time. For New York is a city for the far-sighted: there is nothing to focus upon except the vanishing point. My glance encountered only space. It slid over blocks of houses, all alike, and passed unchecked to the misty horizon.   *Jean-Paul Sartre*

Not that you cannot find those cozy little spots that are such a special part of the charm of European cities. Just stroll through Greenwich Village and you'll discover idyllic nooks, fully enclosed courtyards like Grove Court or Patchin Place. Quite unexpectedly you'll stumble on the old cemetery of the Sephardic Synagogue or the Marble Cemetery on Second Street. You'll find cobblestoned mews which once served as the stables and servants' quarters, and even uptown there are old and new oases of green shade and cool water preserved amid the battlements of cement and glass. But although New York has its smaller, more intimate side, the quintessence of the city, what makes it different from all other world capitals, is its passion for the large-scale. These grand proportions, this sense of expanding space, seem to demand the same kind of format from the people who live and work here, be they business-men or artists.

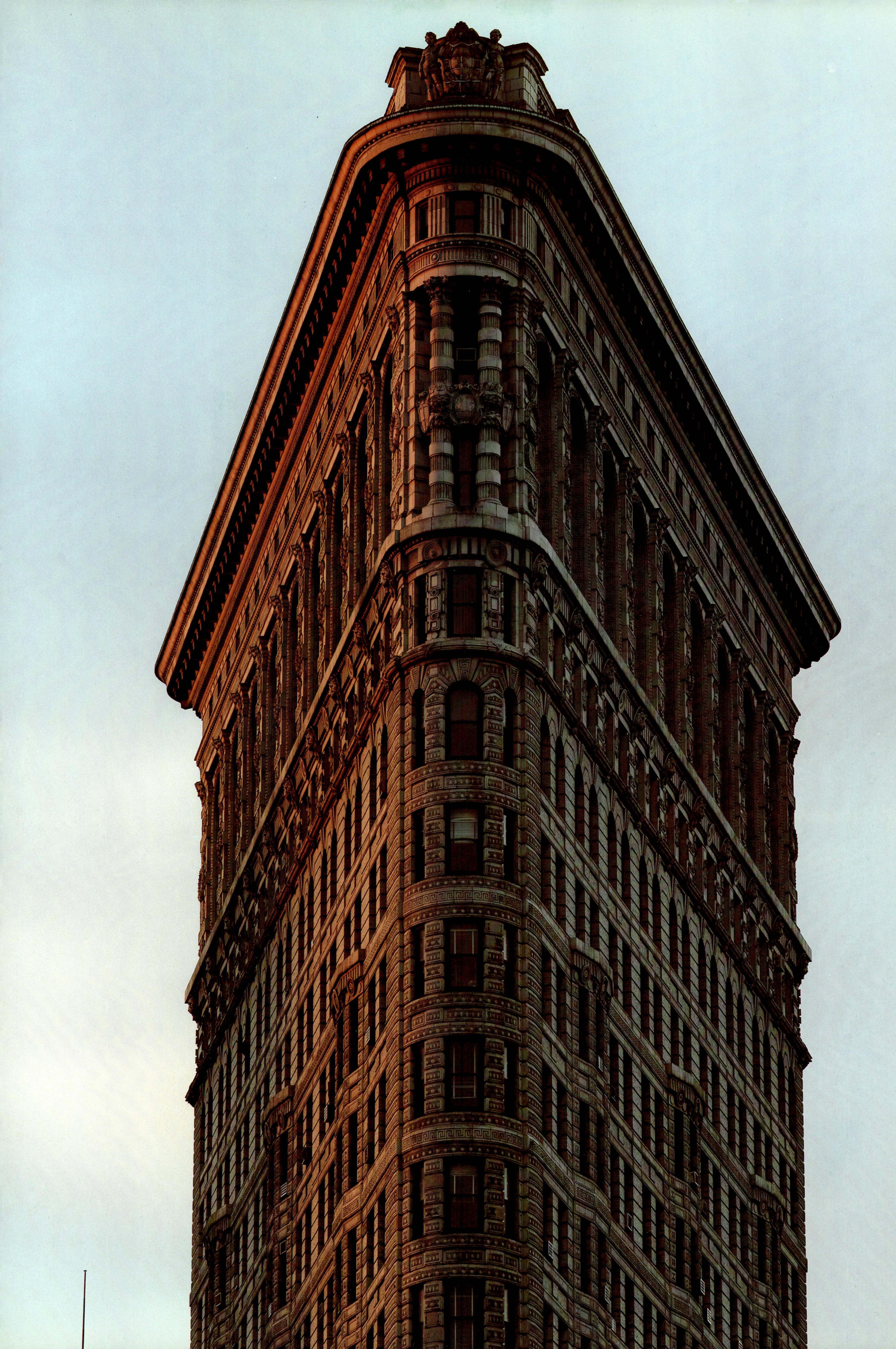

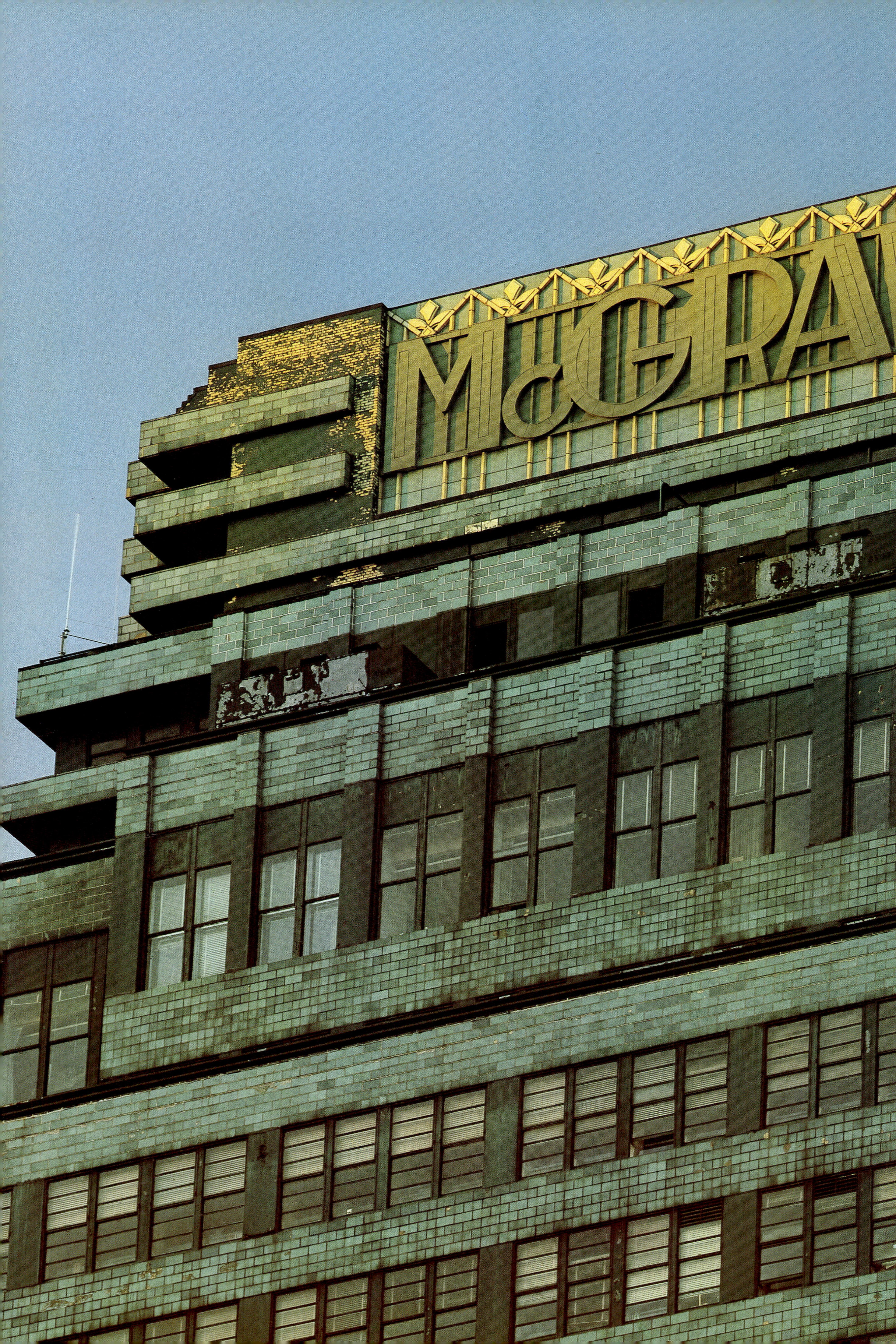

McGRA

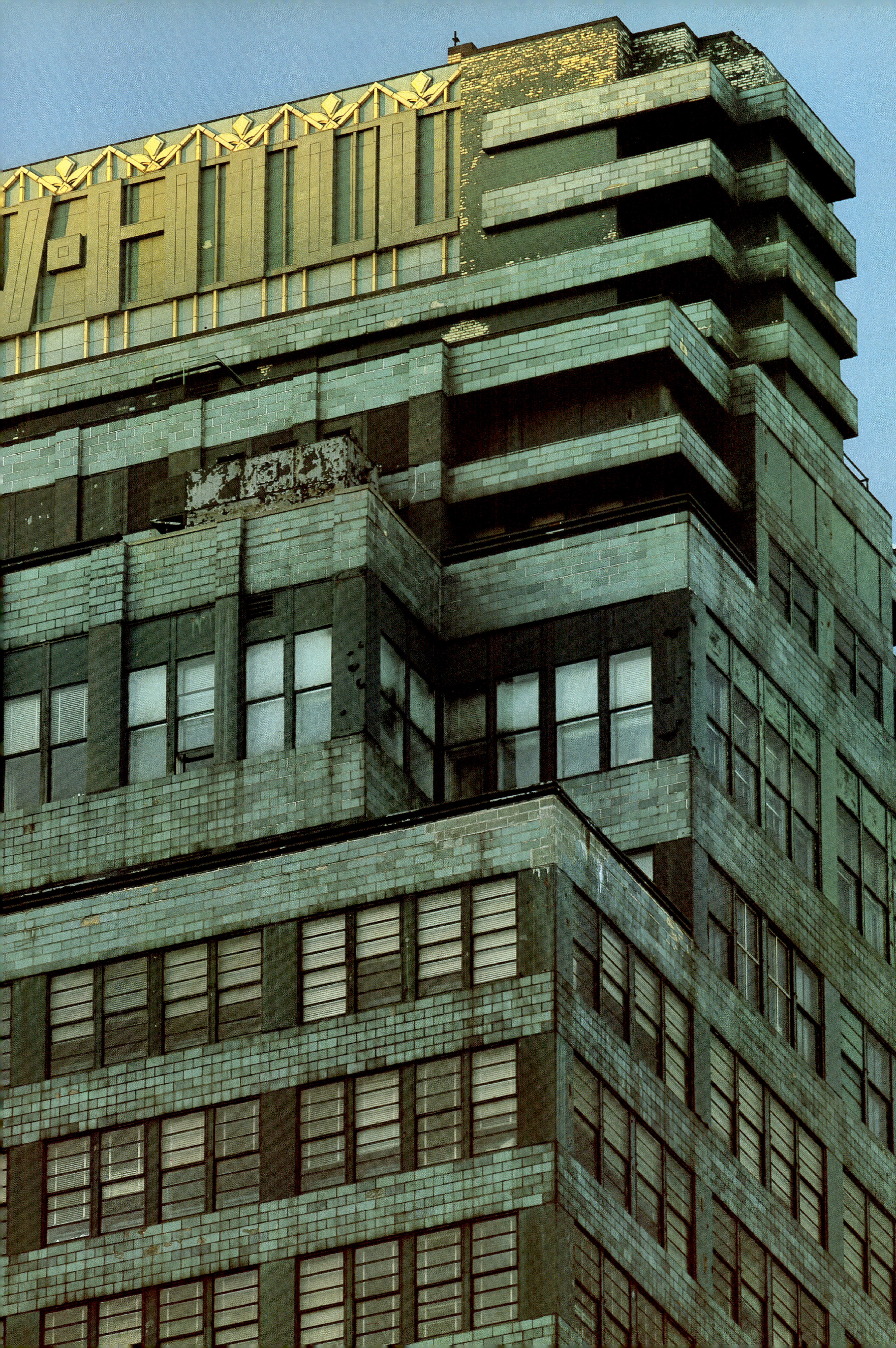

Louise Nevelson

The businessman feels the challenge of the city as well. New York is the financial capital of the world, the hub of the world's markets. Here both ideas and goods are exchanged; what was produced elsewhere is here assigned a value on the market and is traded from hand to hand. Detroit is the motor city of America, Pittsburgh the heart of its steel industry, Texas the state with the oil – but they all depend on New York City for the financial backing that makes everything possible and on the admen of Madison Avenue who can prettify their wares. In a city of skyscrapers the businessman must necessarily think high, think big. The projected plans are larger, the risks to be taken greater than elsewhere, and whoever decides he wants to join in with the others must be ready to meet the demands the city makes of him.

It was the engineer's art that gave the city its silhouette, its skyline – a word coined in the 1890's. At that time, however, the lines being drawn against the sky still took their external form from European models. The Woolworth Building from 1913 assaulted the heavens as pure gothic, complete with gargoyles and caryatids. This Cathedral of Commerce was not received with unanimous applause by its contemporaries; to one critic the very dimensions seemed to sound the alarm that the city was about to become a place of shameless ostentation, "Nineveh and Babylon piled on imperial Rome".

The behemoths which then soon began to fill the skies above Manhattan led to the first New York zoning laws. The Zoning Resolution of 1916 ushered in the terraced look, as exhibited by whole blocks of midtown architecture. Like the steps of a ziggurat, the upper floors of many buildings take a staircase climb into the sky.

Woolworth had commissioned his architect, Cass Gilbert, to build in the style of the British Houses of Parliament. Within a generation, America had found its

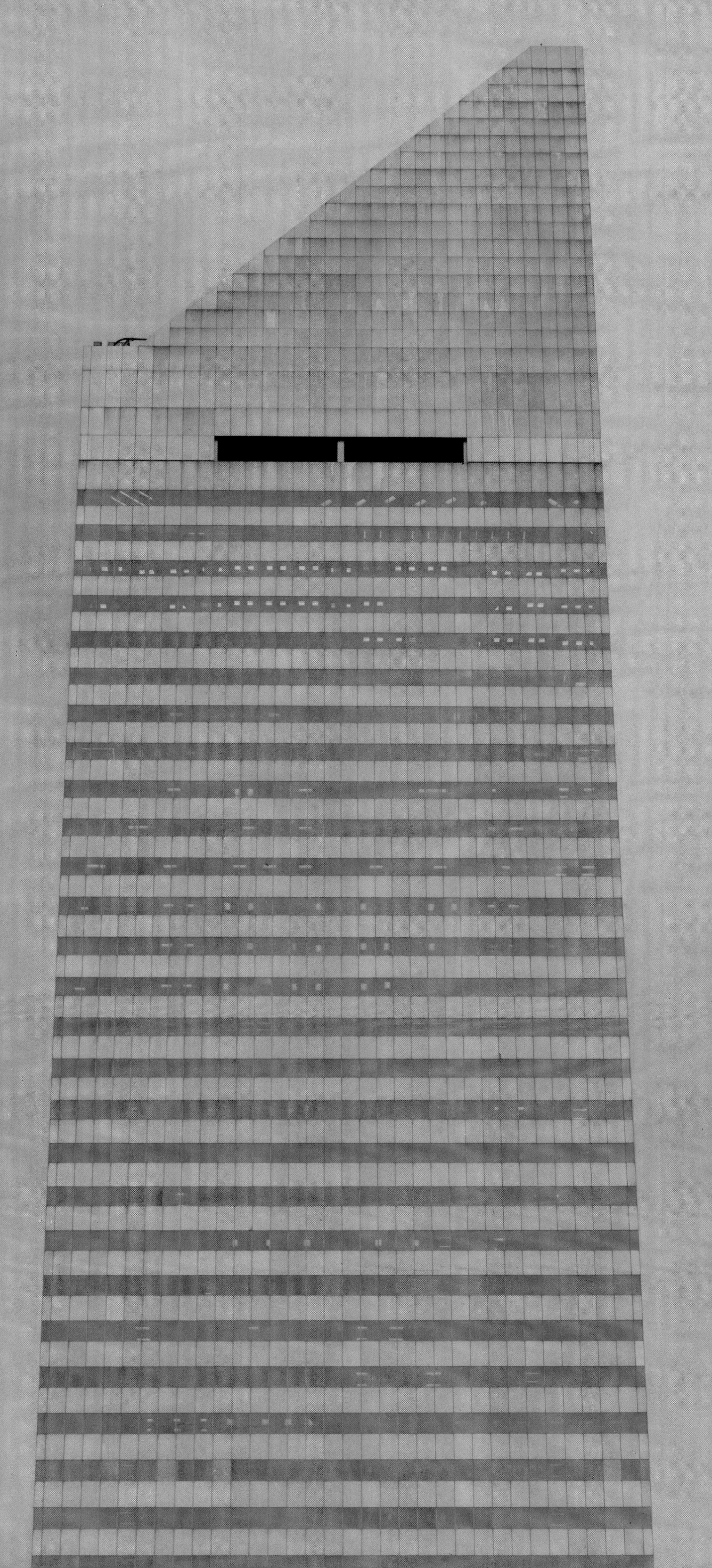

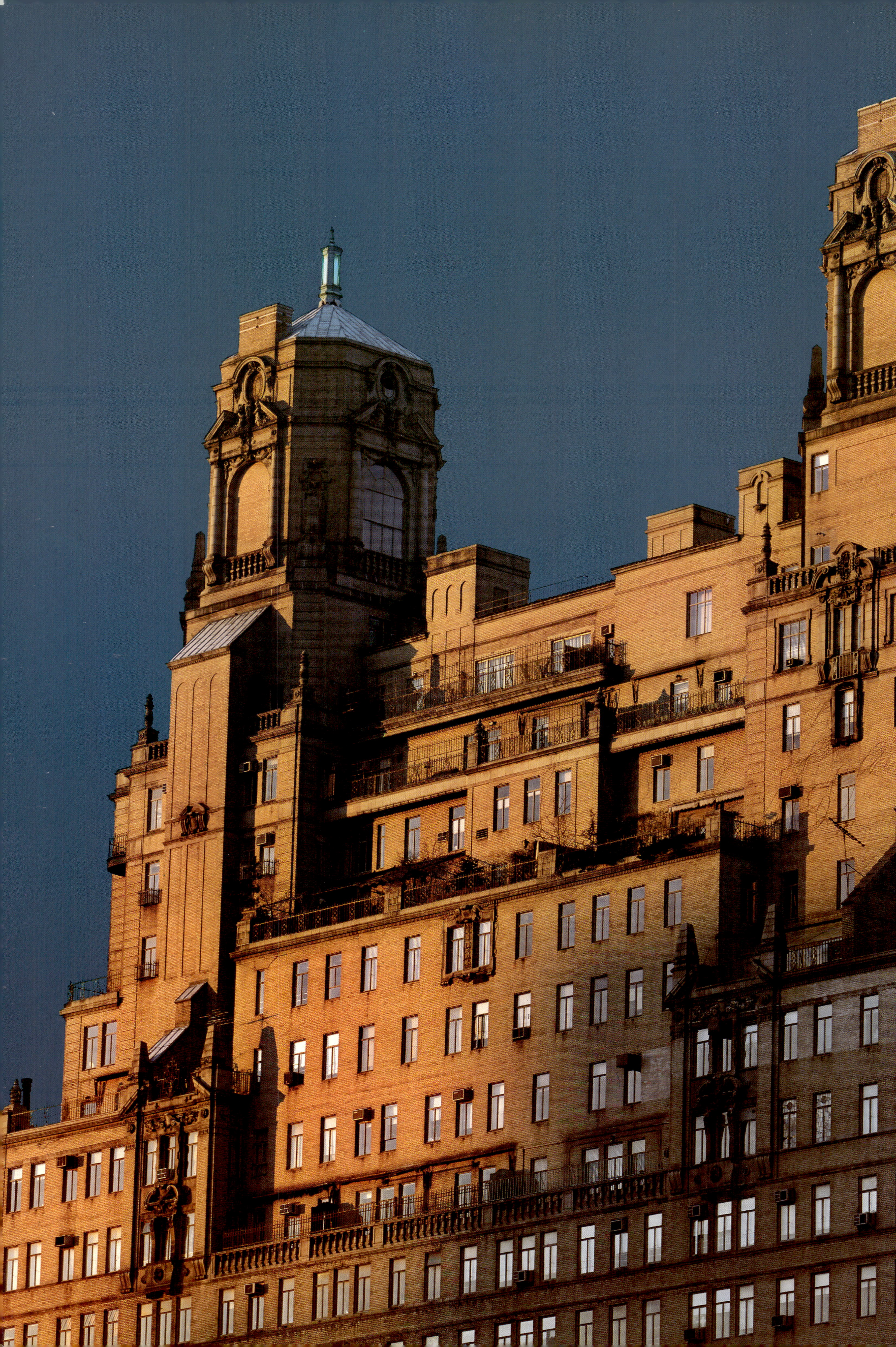

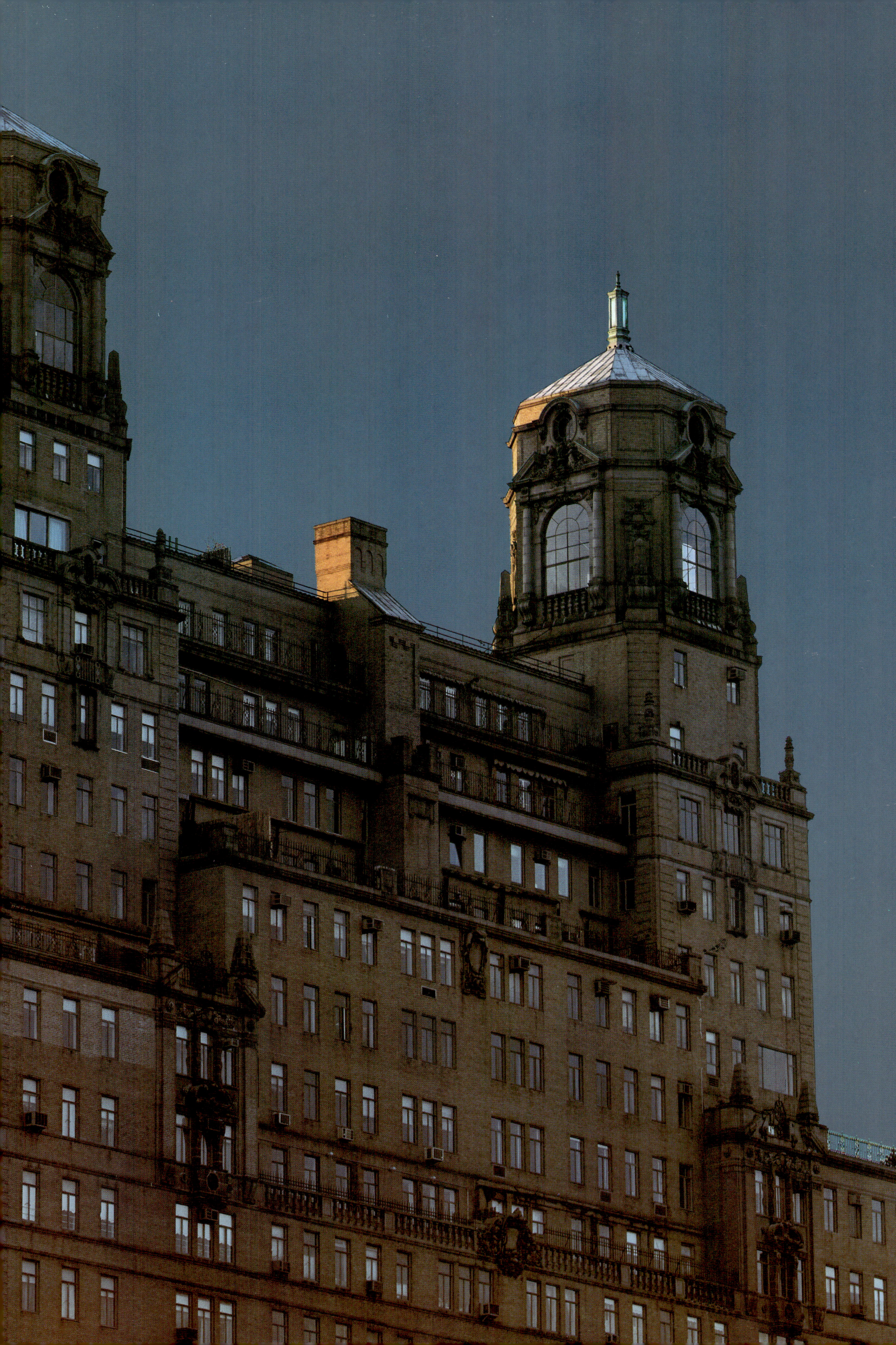

own functional style and no longer needed to camouflage its buildings as cathedrals and palaces. The style of the thirties was the creation of engineers, and it is America's most original contribution to the history of architecture. The builder of the Empire State Building, a politician named Raskob, did not waste his time thumbing through tomes illustrating famous edifices of the past; he stood a number two pencil end up on his desk blotter and asked his architect, "Bill, how high can you make it so that it won't fall down?" That year, 1929, this new variety of stone asparagus was growing everywhere, each shoot higher than the next, in hot competition for every additional inch.

Trying to outtrump their rivals by a yard or two, construction workers would keep pinnacles and antennae hidden in the elevator shafts till the last minute before they were to be mounted. In order to beat out the Chrysler Building, Raskob added on another five stories and stuck on a mast that was supposed to serve as an anchor for zeppelins – never used, of course. When on May 1st, 1931, President Hoover pushed the button in the White House which turned on the lights of this newest of New York skyscrapers, the Empire State Building with its 1250 feet was the tallest structure in the world.

The shimmering pinnacles of thirties architecture are slender and functional, the apotheosis of a technical age. Even the decor glorifies technology: the metallic scales on the roof of the Chrysler Building simulate the design of automobile hubcaps. The crown of the General Electric Building is bathed at night in bottle-green light, and the vertical pillars of the office of the Daily News are vigorous stripes of brown and white brick. It was the age of Art Deco, a movement ignited by the Paris Exposition des Arts Décoratifs in 1925. Ceramic tile and streamlined metal arranged in wild zigzags and geometric figures, jungles of golden vegetation and supple birds – they overran the restaurants, the movie theaters, the nightclubs, even the great public buildings like Rockefeller Center. In this new generation of skyscrapers Art Deco found its coolest, most rigorous and lasting expression.

In retrospect these glittering towers impress us now as belated exclamation points for the "Roaring Twenties". The Depression left many floors in these buildings standing empty for the first years of their lives. One mammoth project was obstinately brought to completion despite such adversity: construction on Rockefeller Center, planned in

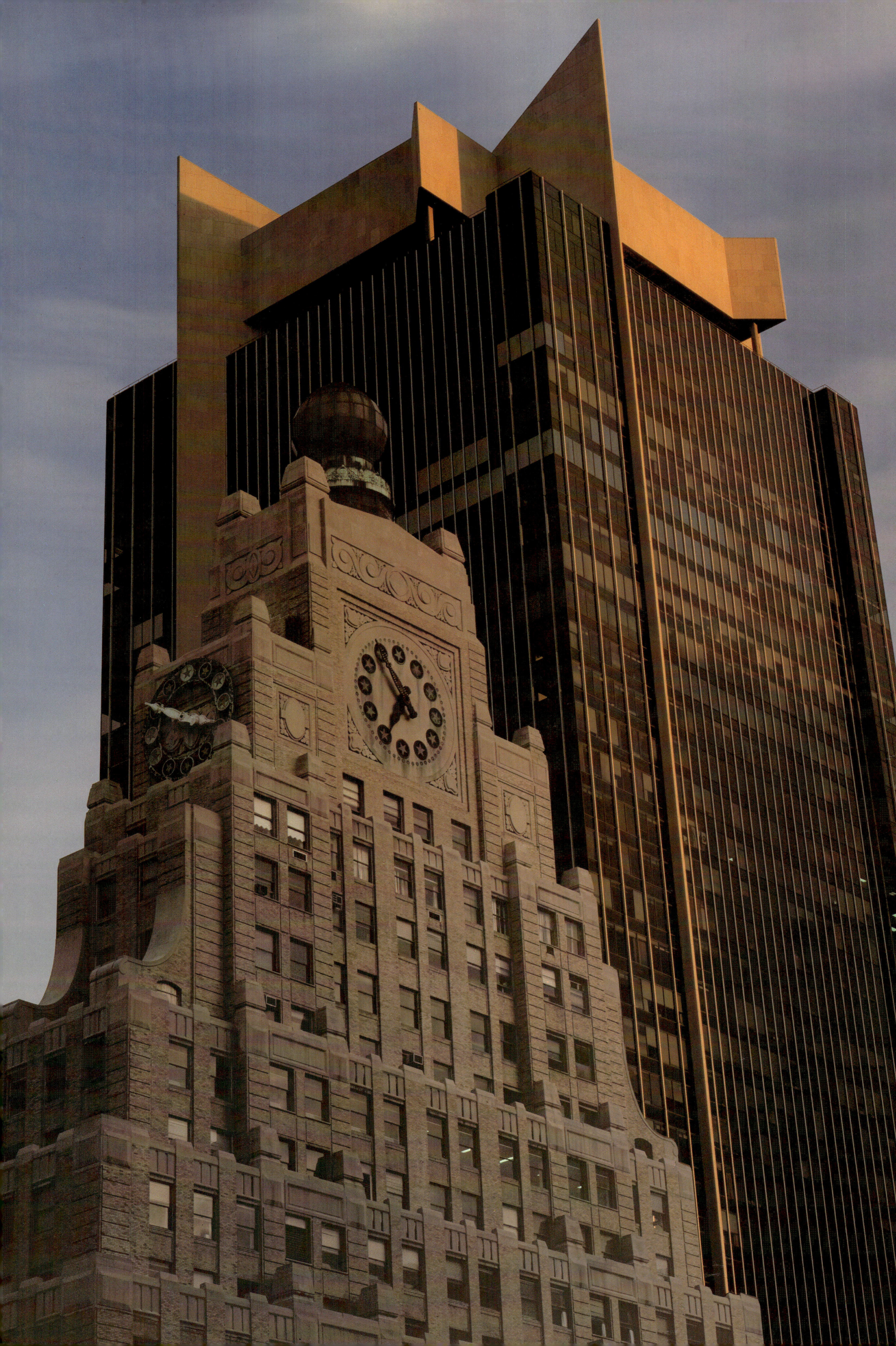

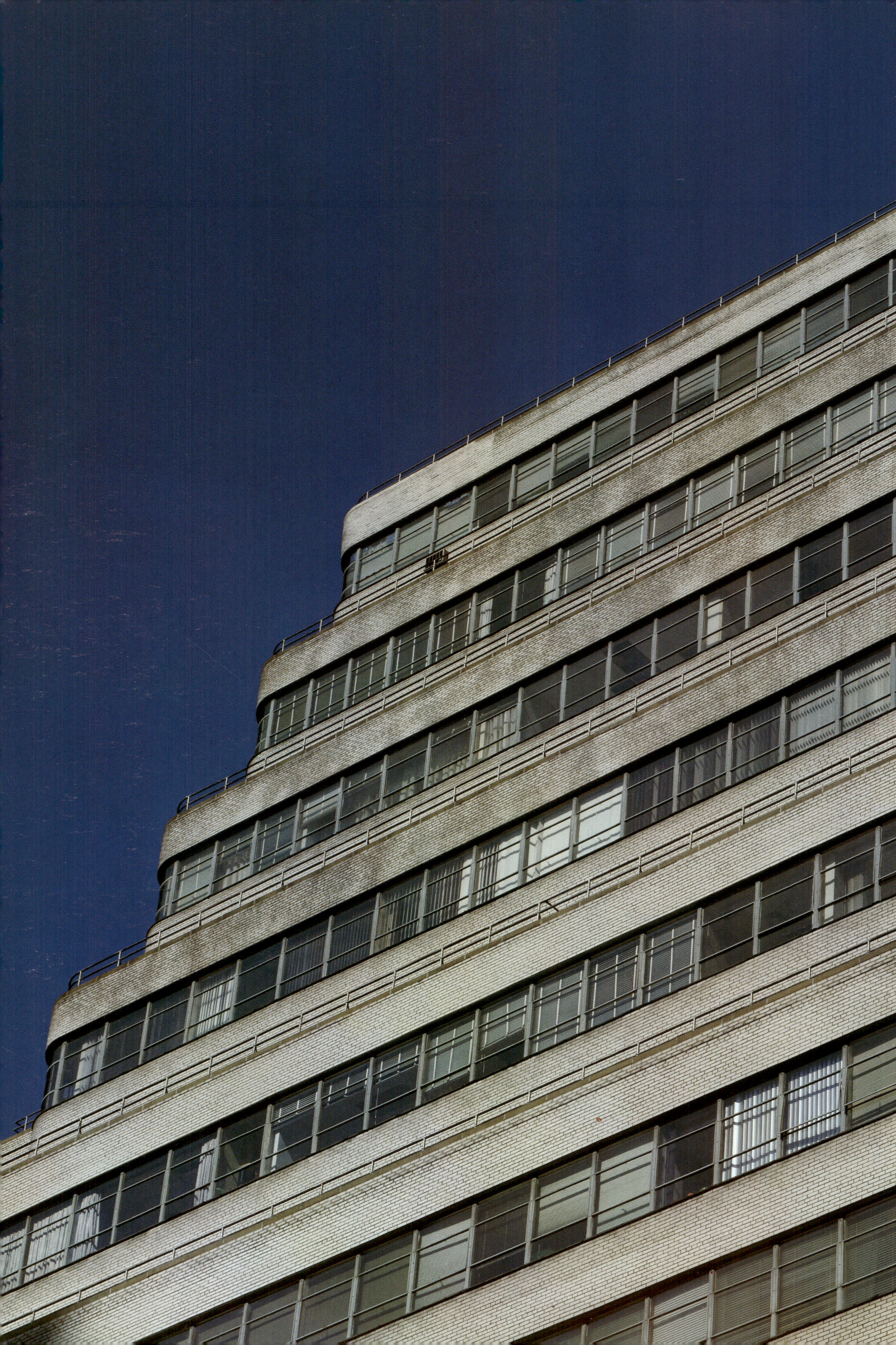

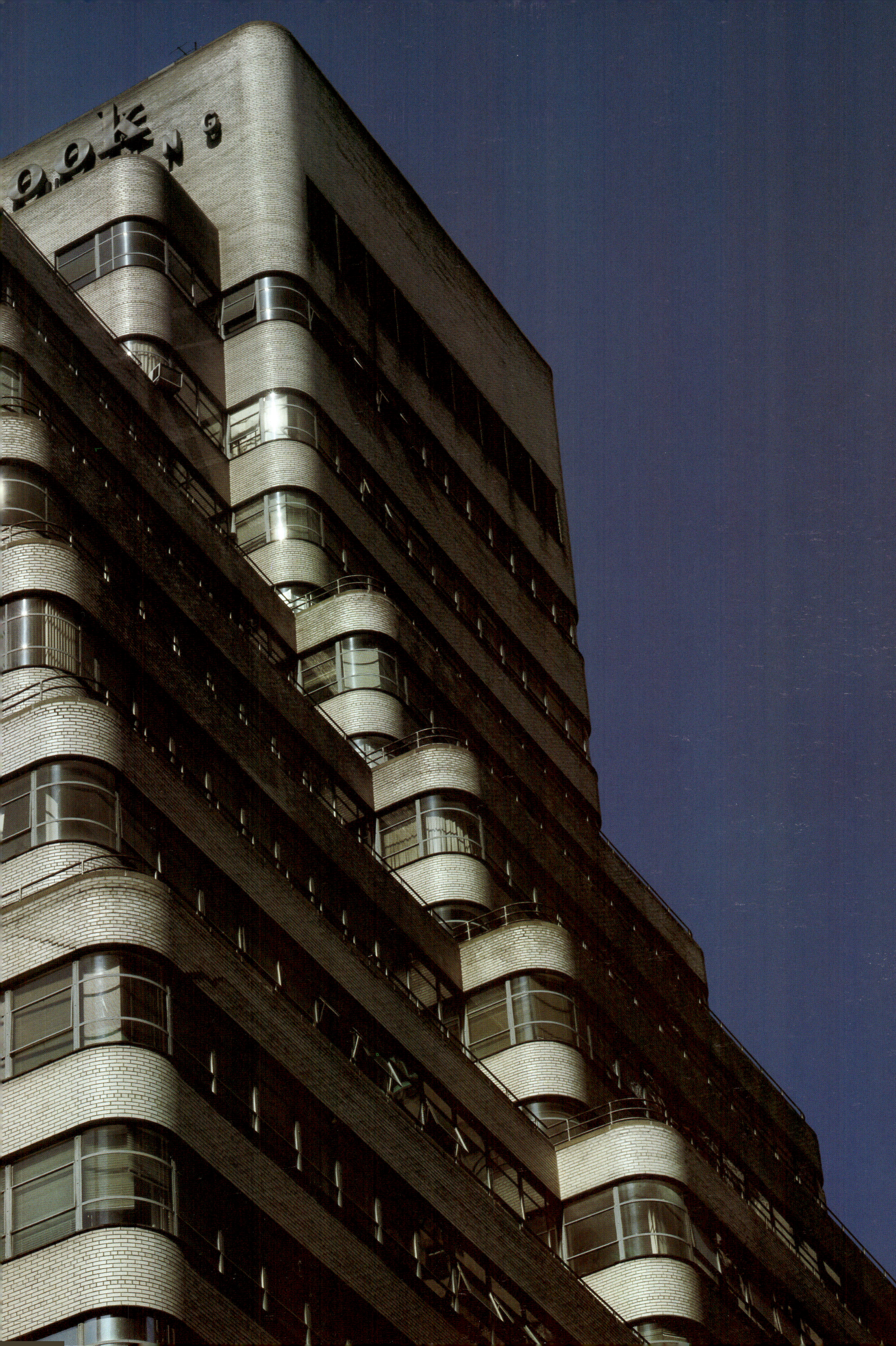

1929, continued through two decades, with the first major section completed in 1947. It is the prototype of the city-within-a-city, a living organic whole, where work and recreation are united. At its center, ringed by office towers and restaurants, is the ice-skating rink where a giant Christmas tree stands in winter and which converts into a flower-bedecked garden café in summer – a veritable oasis for central Manhattan. Like some limestone mountain range, dwarfing the gothic spires of St. Patrick's Cathedral across Fifth Avenue, it rises up in the heart of New York. From the observation deck of the RCA tower you can let your eyes roam across the vastness of the city, rivers and sea – on clear days as far as sixty miles up the majestic Hudson.

Different building periods have lent New York a variety of forms and colors, and a single block may often display several of them in a jumble. For the first two centuries of its history the steep-roofed brick houses of the Dutch who founded it gave New York its dominant color, red – just as Paris is silvery gray and Rome orange. In the middle of the nineteenth century a brownish-violet chocolate coating began to melt over everything: "brownstone", a soft, fine-grained sandstone easily shaped into the pedestals and consoles, oriels and ornaments that the Italianate mode of the period demanded of every façade.

Ultimately, however, it was neither red brick nor the darker brownstone, nor even the glass curtain-walls of the office-lined boulevards bequeathed by the Bauhaus which became the hallmark of New York. For more than all these others it is still the skyscrapers of the thirties which stick in our memories as "classic New York". Without doubt they have met stiff competition from the sharp-edged boxes of glass and steel which, ever since Mies van der Rohe's Seagram Building of 1958, have been transforming the center of the city and which, as the sixties progressed, crowded out more and more of the arabesques and filigree from the skyline. But contemporary New York seems now to have grown tired of these cheap, mass-produced copies of Bauhaus functionalism. The most recent buildings have quite unexpectedly taken to adding elements of fantasy to the rigorous architecture demanded till now by corporate America – and we are once again being treated to that playfulness which has marked New York architecture through all its periods. The very latest towers are ready to provide "camp" ornamentation and ironic detail.

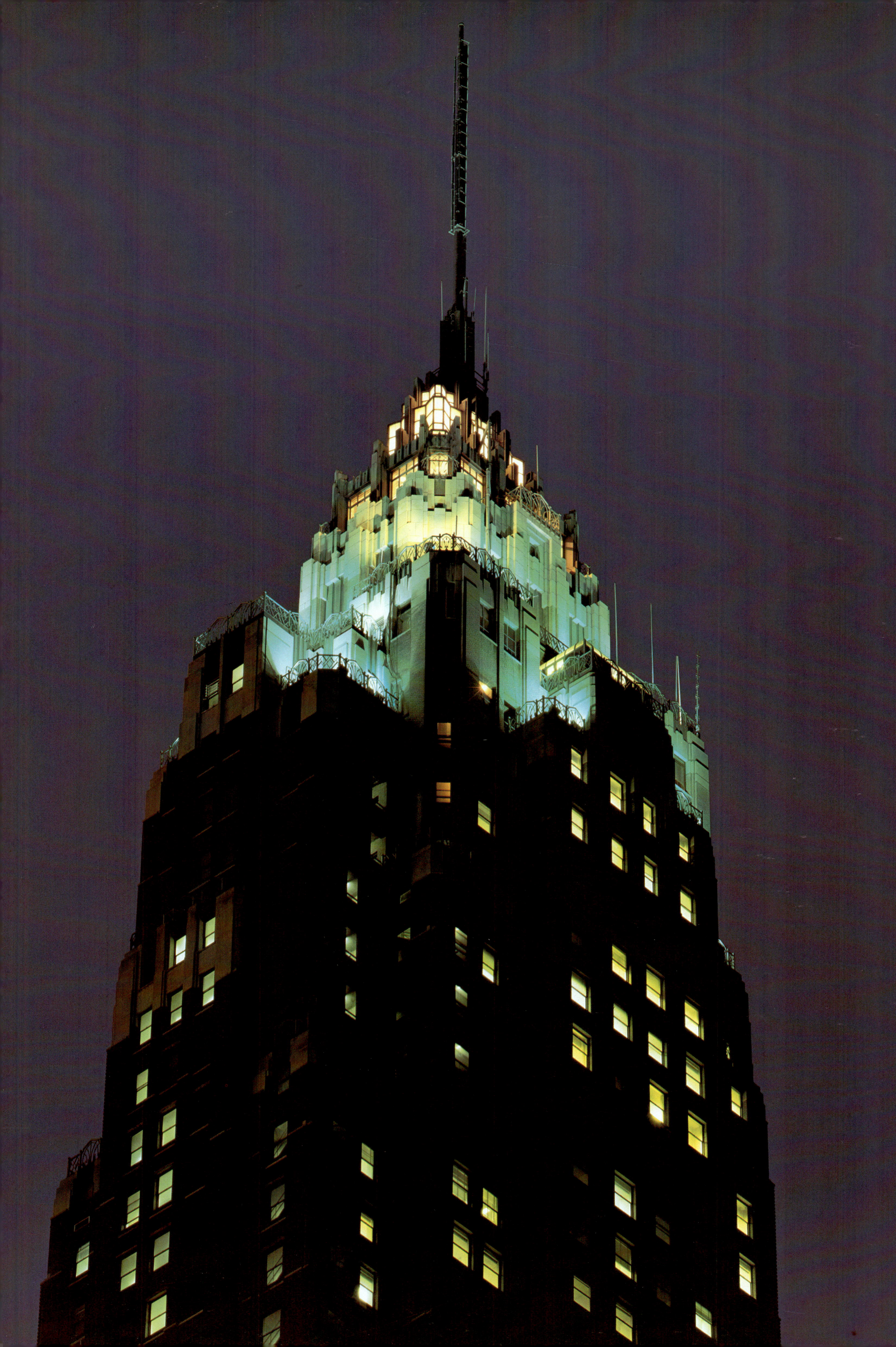

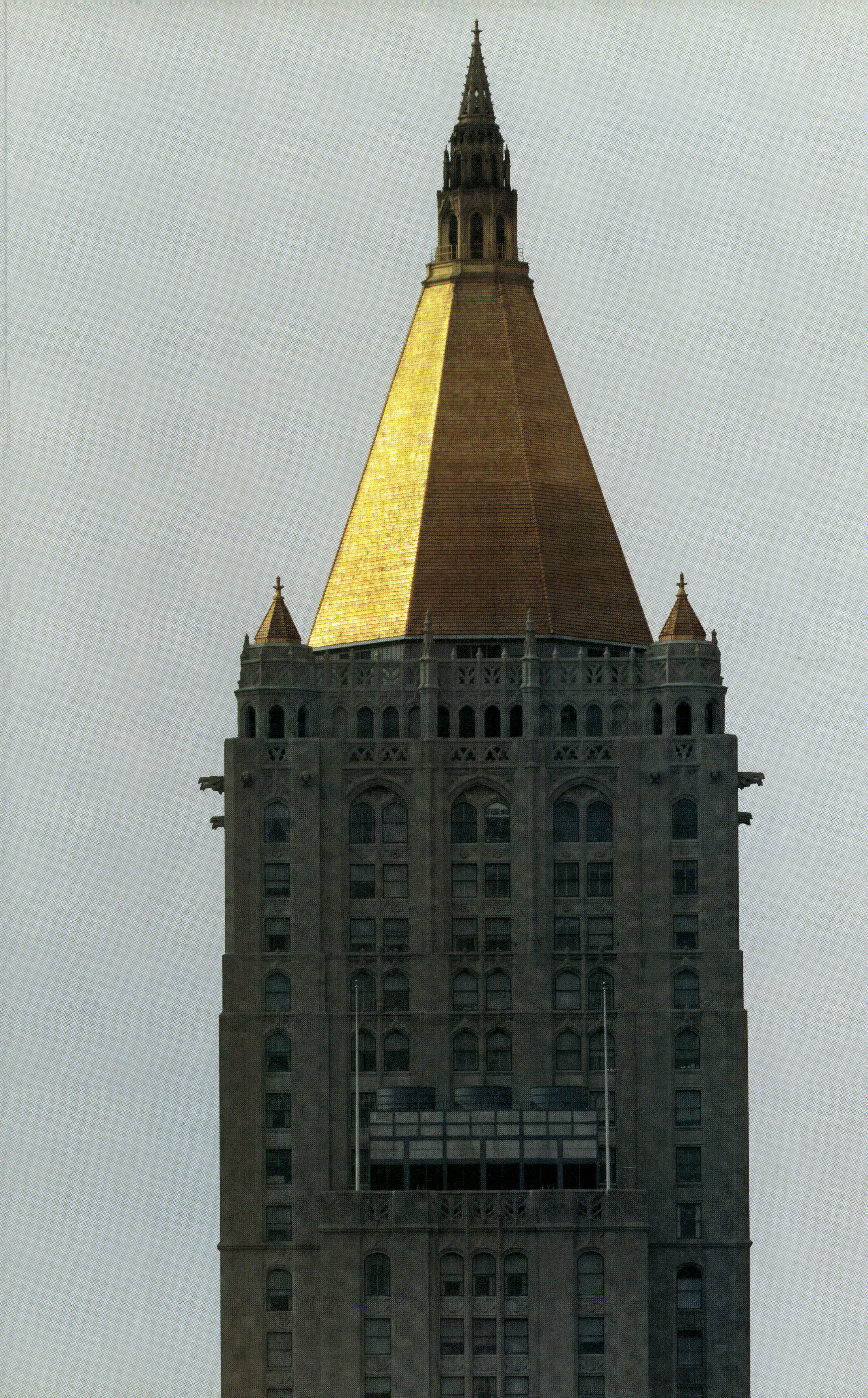

Philip Johnson, for instance, one of the heralds of the International Style who worked with Mies on the Seagram Building, has designed the new headquarters of American Telephone and Telegraph with a curlicued "chippendale" gable at the top. On cold days the exhaust steam of the heating system will, it is planned, come puffing out of the hole in the middle. Johnson senses that there has been a change in the public's taste:

We stand at an enormous watershed. We stand at a place where maybe we haven't stood for fifty years, and that is a shift in sensibility so revolutionary that it is hard to grasp because we are right in the middle of it. It is the watershed between what we have all been brought up with as the Modern, and something new, uncharted, uncertain and absolutely delightful.   *Philip Johnson*

And so New York remains faithful to its striking characteristic, the longing for constant change and the talent to effect it. It all confirms the vision Le Corbusier saw of the white cathedral that is never finished, of the geyser whose fountains leap and gush in continual renewal. This city denies what yesterday was written about it. Today's new building is tomorrow's ruin. With that boundless energy that is its special mark, New York regenerates with every generation. Each farewell becomes a new beginning and every pile of rubble turns into humus for a forest of new spires. In spite of all the prophecies of doom, New York delights in the rapture of survival, a joy which it imparts to its citizens. The city is a durable behemoth, the Capital triumphant over all Cassandras.

Sabina Lietzmann
New York, May 1980

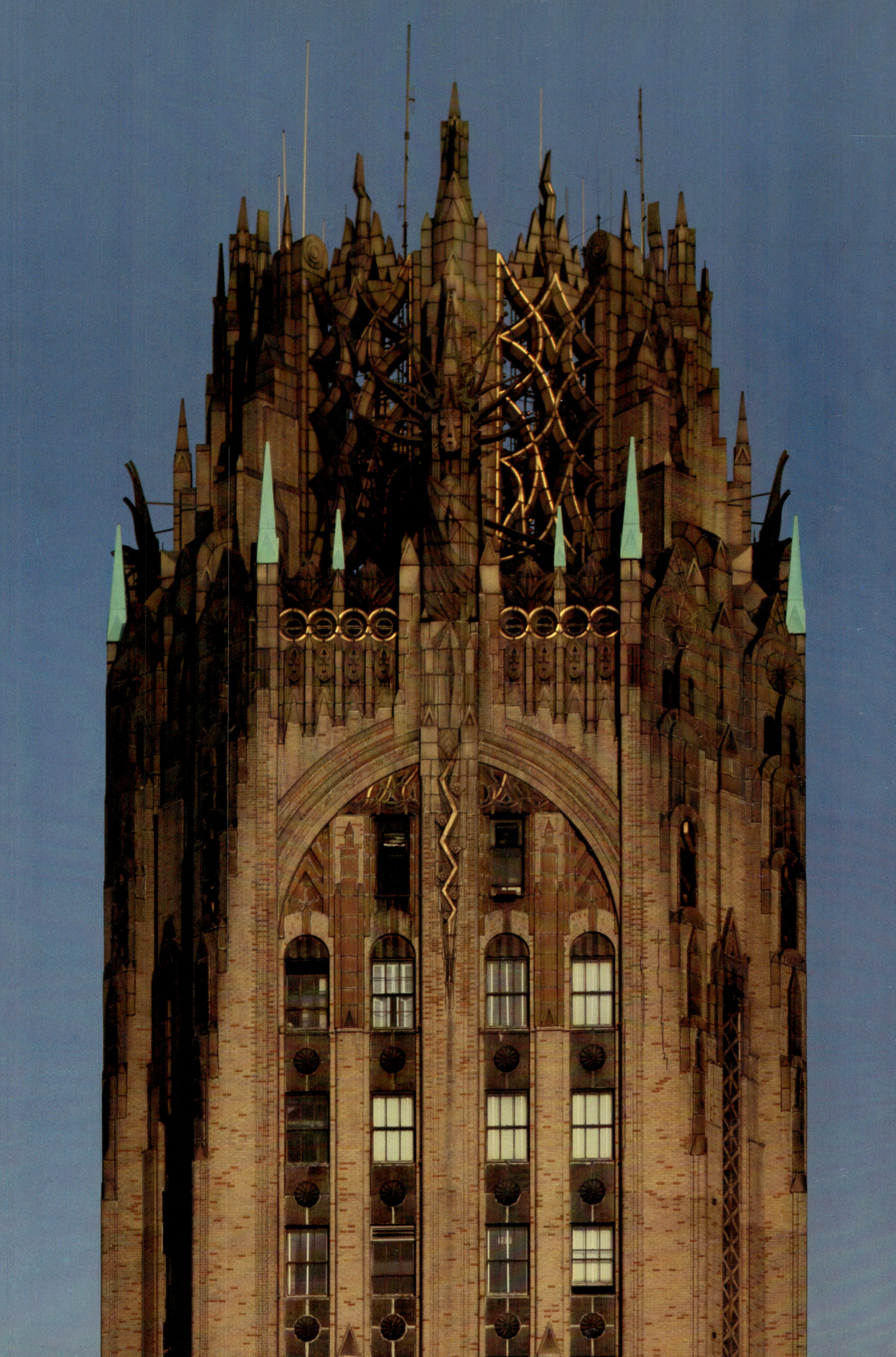

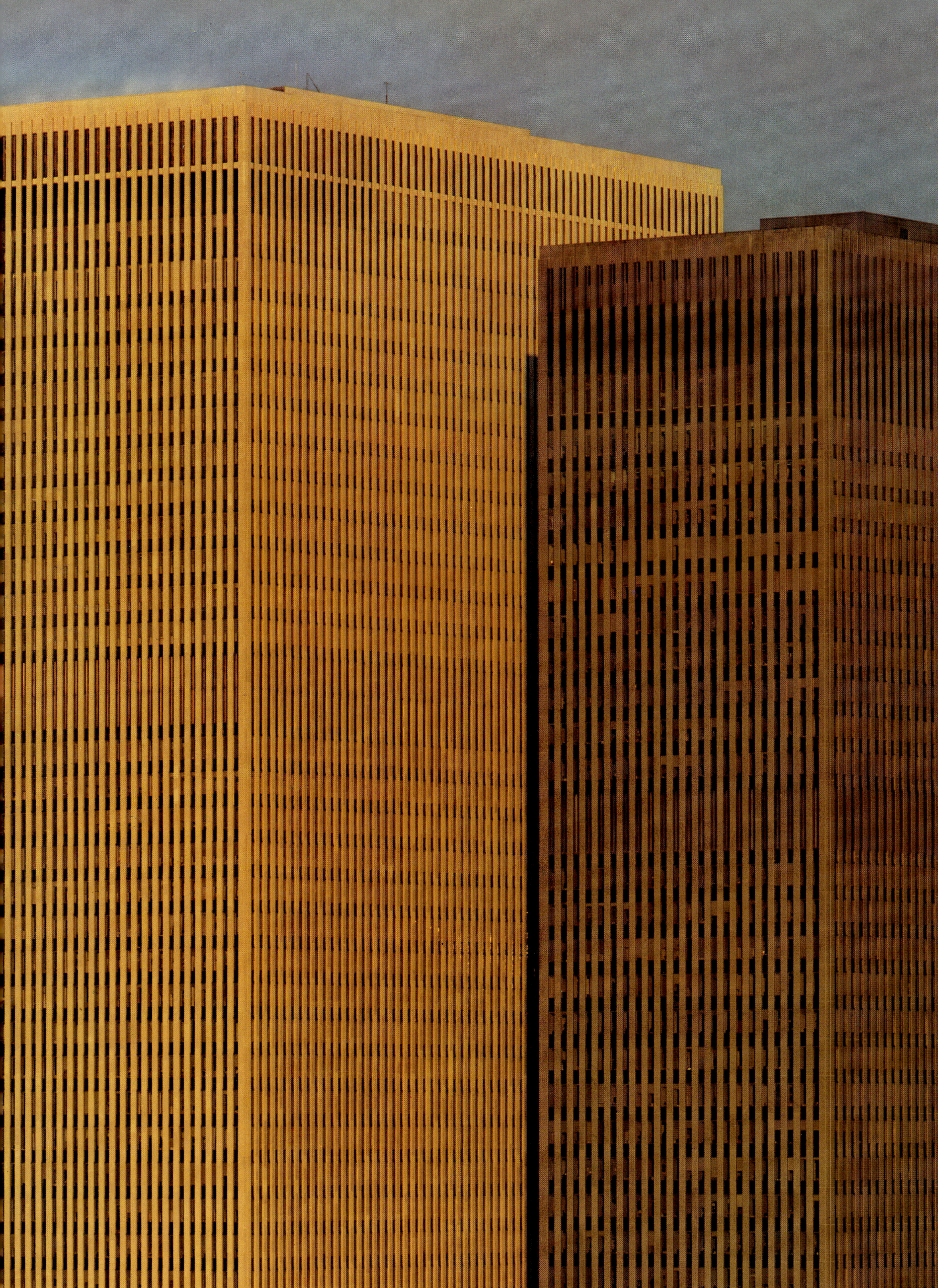

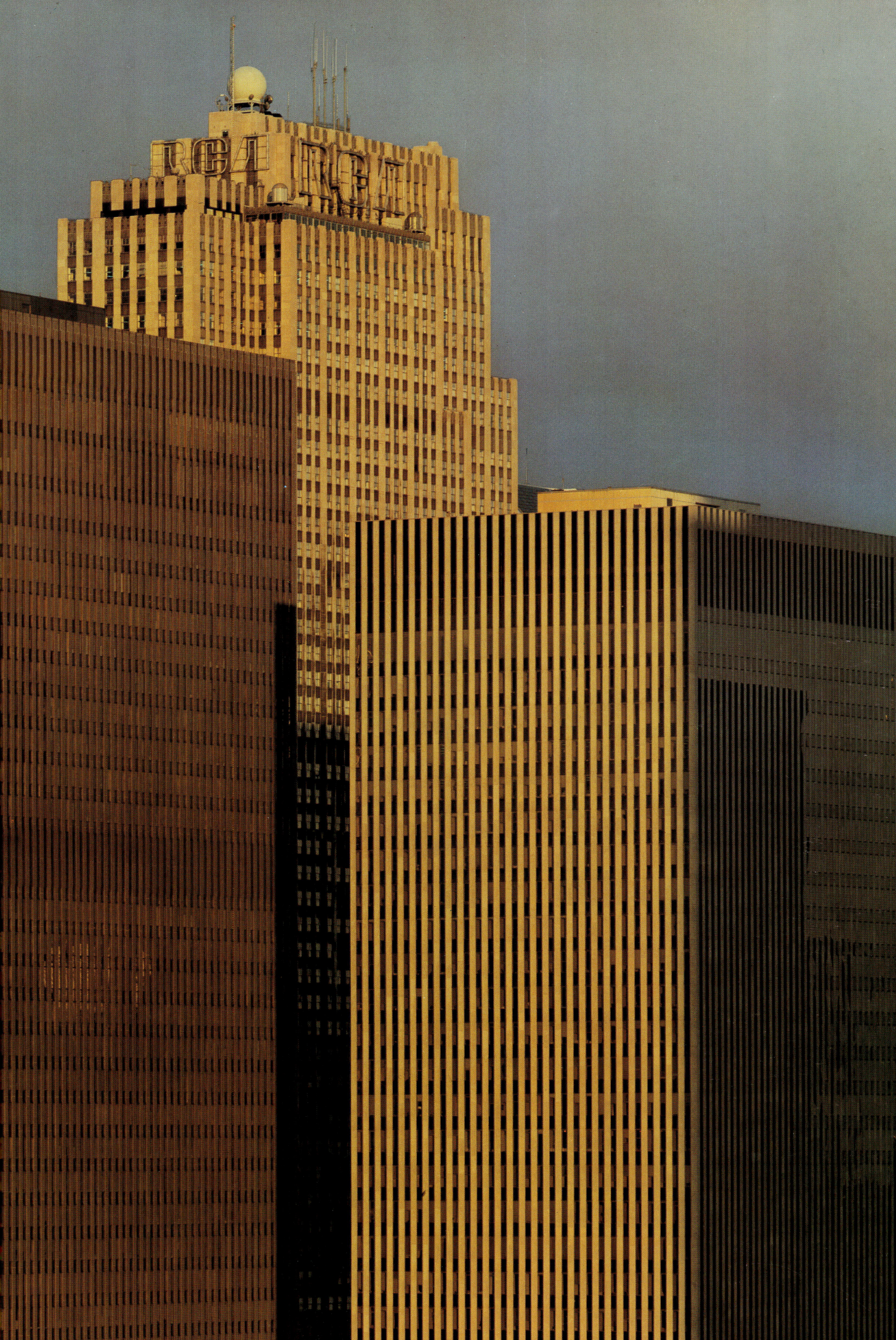

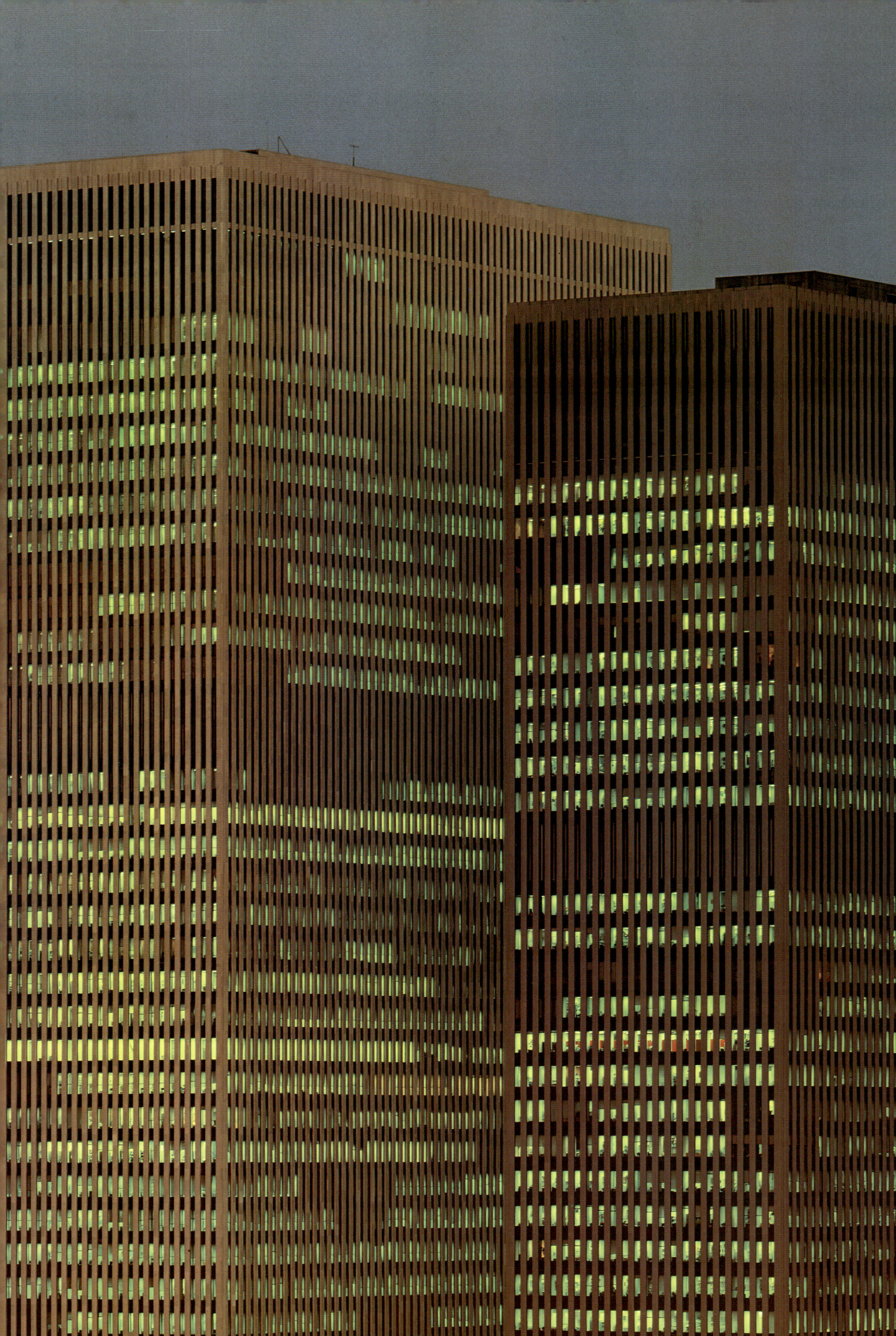

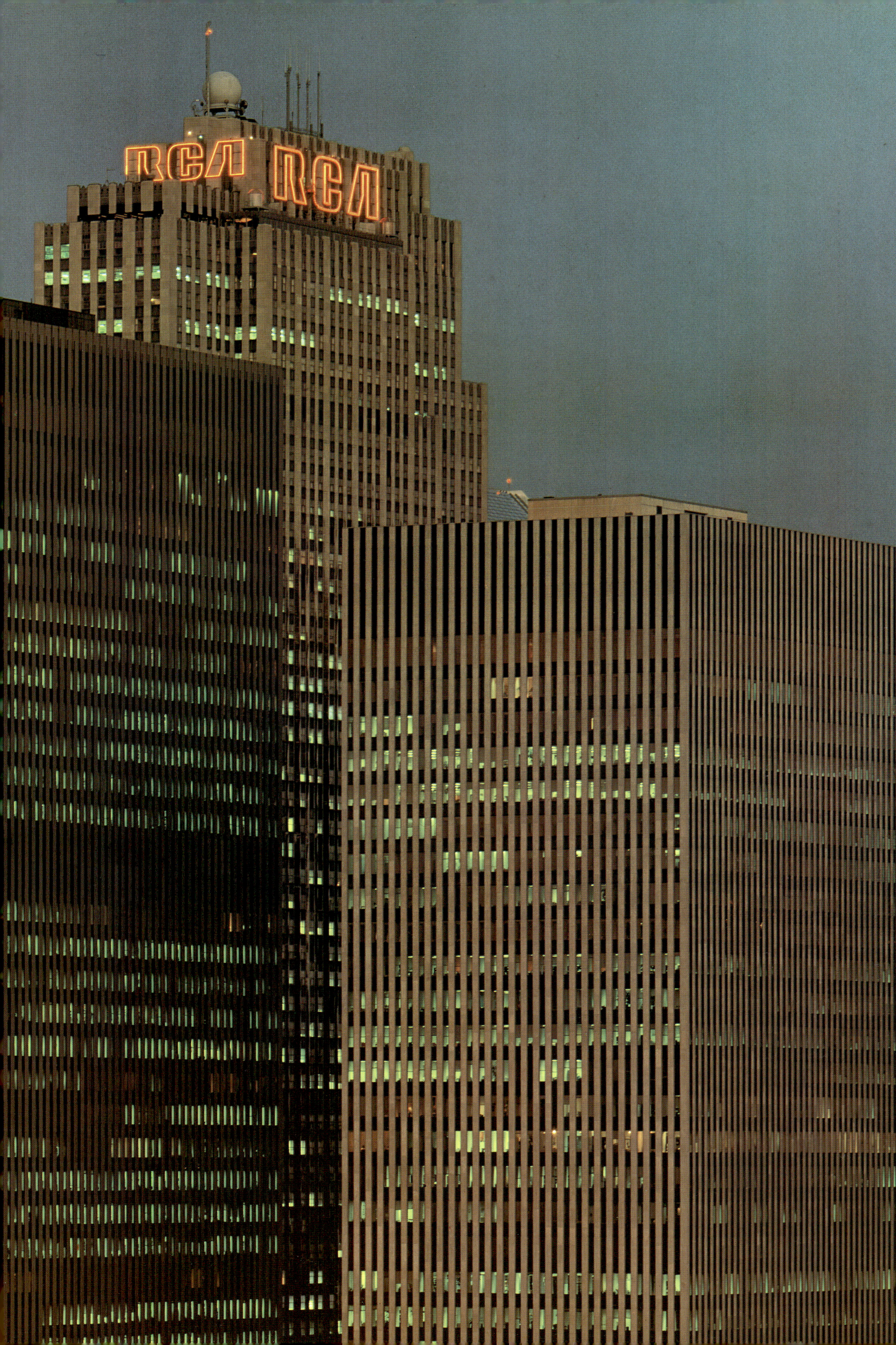

RCA RCA

Andy Warhol:
Interview with Reinhart Wolf, New York, April 30th, 1980

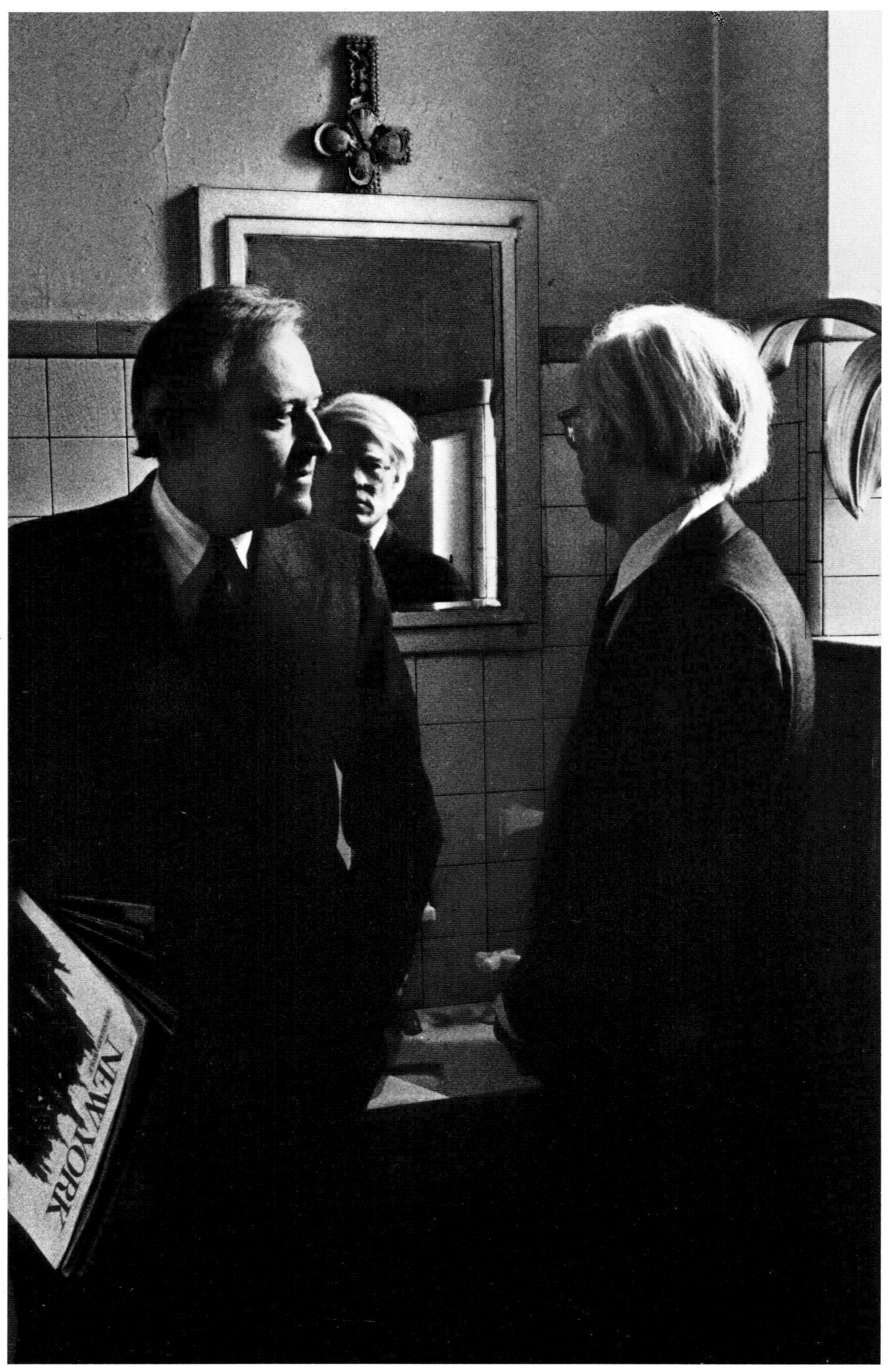

PHOTO: HENRY WOLF.

A. W.:   Reinhart, why did you do New York instead of Hollywood? I like
Hollywood better.

R. W.:   I can understand that, Andy, but you must admit that Hollywood is sort
of flat – and I like tops. I really feel that the tops of New York's
skyscrapers express the strength and the spirit of America. New York
inspires me – the skyscrapers are like phallic symbols of fertility. I
wanted to capture these buildings before they disappear. Now
construction is going on everywhere I look. Many of the buildings I've
wanted to photograph have already been demolished.

A. W.:   You make New York look so different: all mixed-up.

R. W.:   New York i s mixed-up! The confusion of styles can even be mad and
dynamic! And it is exactly this which demonstrates the creative power of
the city. And besides – something is really certain, I think: the people
who erected these buildings were all trying for one thing: to defy the
stars!

A. W.:   Why did you do these photographs? Was it an assignment for a
magazine?

R. W.:   Actually it was an assignment. It was the idea of a friend of mine,
Thomas Höpker, editor of GEO magazine. We were looking at buildings
from his office window on the 33rd floor on Park Avenue when he said:
"Reinhart, just take a look at these delightful pinnacles, and to think
that hardly anybody ever even notices them! Why don't you photograph
them for us?" And this I did.

A. W.:   Are these photographs for everybody or just architects?

R. W.:   For everybody, of course! I wanted to open people's eyes, to get them to
         look up. And I hope I've succeeded. Everybody who has seen these photo-
         graphs so far walks around New York trying to find more. People might
         begin noticing small details and also grasp the whole in new and
         surprising ways. The beauty of all that architecture really leads to disco-
         veries, almost like new trips!

A. W.:   It must have been very difficult to take these pictures. I don't think I
         could take them.

R. W.:   Well, it was hard work. I used a big 8 by 10 camera so as to capture the
         smallest detail with the greatest possible precision; and I used a long
         focal-length lens supported by two heavy tripods, sometimes – when
         there was wind – even anchored in position with rocks. In addition my
         assistant and I had to carry five heavy cases with all the necessary
         equipment. However, the most difficult thing was to persuade people to
         let us on to their roofs, even to just have a look. I spent hours,
         sometimes days convincing doormen, building managers, superinten-
         dents and tenants that my intentions were legitimate. And then the
         shock when I said 5 a.m.! That's when we usually started setting up to
         catch the first rays of the beautiful morning light. And the endless
         pleadings and checking that certain lights be turned on in the buildings
         being photographed! And when the morning with the right weather
         finally arrived and my sleepy assistant dropped me off and parked the
         car leaving me with all those cases and tripods in a totally deserted
         street, I just prayed I wouldn't get mugged. And then on our difficult
         journey through revolving doors and into elevators we were always
         viewed with dark suspicion. People were downright scared meeting us
         that early in the morning with what could easily have been the latest
         thing in machine-guns. But once you conquered all these obstacles and
         you got into position on the right roof and your picture was there in
         front of you – in the right distance with the right angle and the right
         sky, – it gave you such an overwhelming feeling of achievement and
         success – downright joy! It was like reaching the summit of Mount
         Everest.

A. W.:   Reinhart, these buildings make me think of money.

R. W.:   You are right. It's the good face of capitalism. It took time and money to
         build them. The men who have erected Manhattan are the Medicis of
         America. They sponsored the best artists and craftsmen of their time
         and took advantage of their talents. A marvellous and useful way of
         spending big money.

A. W.:   Reinhart, do you only take photographs of buildings?

R. W.:   No. I started by taking portraits of painters and sculptors in Paris. Then
         I went into advertising where I did everything from coffeebeans to
         airplanes. But I have always been interested in architecture, coming
         from a family of architects. And then ten years ago I started to
         photograph buildings which became to be like human faces for me.

A. W.:   I think architecture and photography are the two big arts now. All the
         kids we know want to be either architects or photographers – or models.
         Why didn't you become an architect? Or a model?

R. W.:   I like being *behind* the camera: I think it gives you more command.
         And as far as architecture is concerned, I would hate the idea of having
         to face my mistakes my whole life long! If I take a bad picture, I can just
         tear it up.

A. W.:   How did you pick the buildings, Reinhart?

R. W.:   With binoculars. I was looking for power, wit, and – for want of a better
         word – something a little camp.

A. W.:   Did you shoot all day and all night?

R. W.:   No, Andy, but it certainly occupied my mind night and day. I usually
         shot at dawn or dusk because I prefer the mood of the light at these
         hours.

A. W.:   Reinhart, I think you're an artist. Do you?

R. W.:   Let me put it like this, Andy: I took these pictures as an "amateur" in
         the purest sense of the word, derived from the Latin "amare", to love: I
         loved what I was doing. Of course my many years as a professional
         photographer have given me the skills, the patience and the discipline
         needed to create these photographs; but to answer your question: I
         think – perhaps – I am an amateur in love with art.

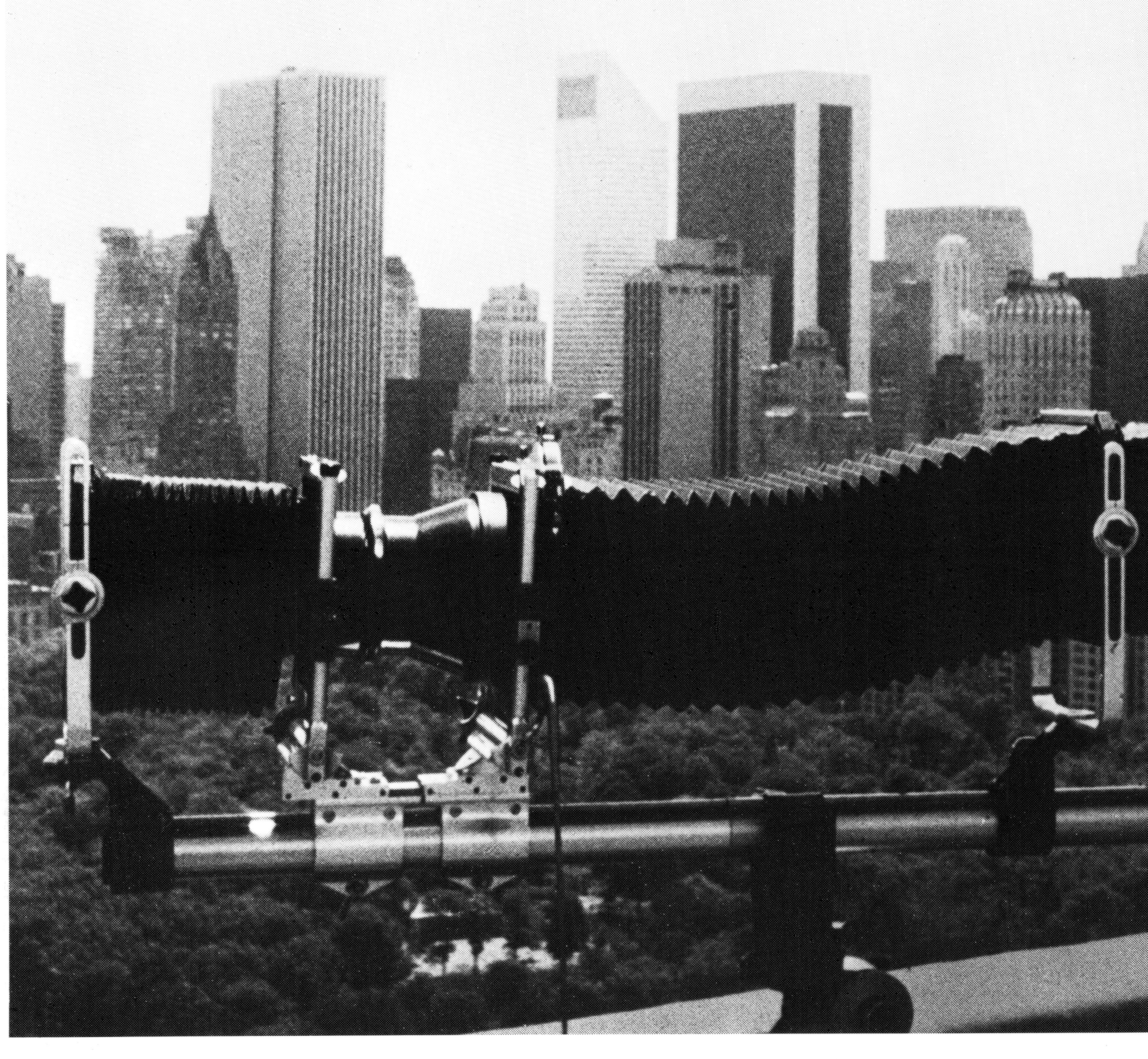

Looking upwards knows no limits (Japanese proverb).

One word cannot encompass art, nor will some single concept ever do the artist justice. The artistic process with its multi-layered structure can only be sketched in fragments and given the gentlest application of color.

For much too long we have believed to be able to express everything with the intellect and its henchman, the word. And what we are left with is merest intimation. Without emotion, without sensibility, there is no understanding.

There are no labels for a personality like Reinhart Wolf's. It is less by descriptive words than by direct personal contact that you come to comprehend him. You must not only speak with Reinhart Wolf, you must see him – if you want to understand what he sees.

Reinhart Wolf's photographic work has been acclaimed on numerous occasions, at exhibitions and congresses of all kinds – not just acclaimed, but discussed in detail as well. Certainly much of that discussion has served to clarify many of the fundamental concepts needed for comprehending his work.

For many years Reinhart Wolf's professional base has been commercial photography – and he is counted among the very best in the trade in Europe. This is the media side of his work – and in it he displays an absolute mastery of his craft.

Commenting on this work, Rainer Fabian wrote in DIE WELT as follows: "Commercial photographers like Reinhart Wolf form one of the most influential groups of our day. But beyond that, Reinhart Wolf has rediscovered something that has been lost to urban civilization since the Renaissance: grace, taste and the kind of culture through which the individual finds his way to a unique style."

A more personal world of expression independent of commissions is articulated both in Reinhart Wolf's early work as a portrait of artists and in later phases, where he has intentionally chosen to portray specific landscapes and buildings. In the many commentaries on this work several points of view merge and lay bare for us the key concepts which also lie behind his work with such a dynamic subject as New York city.

His long-time client from the record industry, his friend Pali Meller Marcovicz, defines Reinhart Wolf's studies of famous men as "faces like landscapes, photographs like paintings" – an analogy which can be easily applied to his study of New York. Meller Marcovicz goes on to write that he has read that Reinhart Wolf creates portraits of objects. "That means he gives a face to things, which is certainly true. For my part, I would not call him a photographer, but rather a director working within his own world of images."

That describes precisely what it is that characterizes Reinhart Wolf's independent work: an inseparable fusion of imagination with a congruity to reality, creating a metamorphosis which is the photographic object.

In an article in the MÜNCHNER MERKUR dealing with the exhibition "Faces of Buildings", Georg Ramseger chose the term "the magic of the commonplace" for what it is that distinguishes this photographic incarnation of an idea. He describes Reinhart Wolf's work with a 8 by 10 camera as a "soundless protest against the inflation of snapshots, as a demonstration against chance and for the deliberately formal picture, for the considered composition, against noise and for quiet."

Reinhart Wolf himself has said, "The picture that appears enlarged upon the focusing screen confronts me as something more serious, more conscious than the small format seen through the single eye of the miniature camera. The first glance at the picture I am planning, when it answers me from the focusing screen, is the moment of truth. The picture which till now I had defined, now defines me."

Fritz Gruber describes the process in another way: "Everything

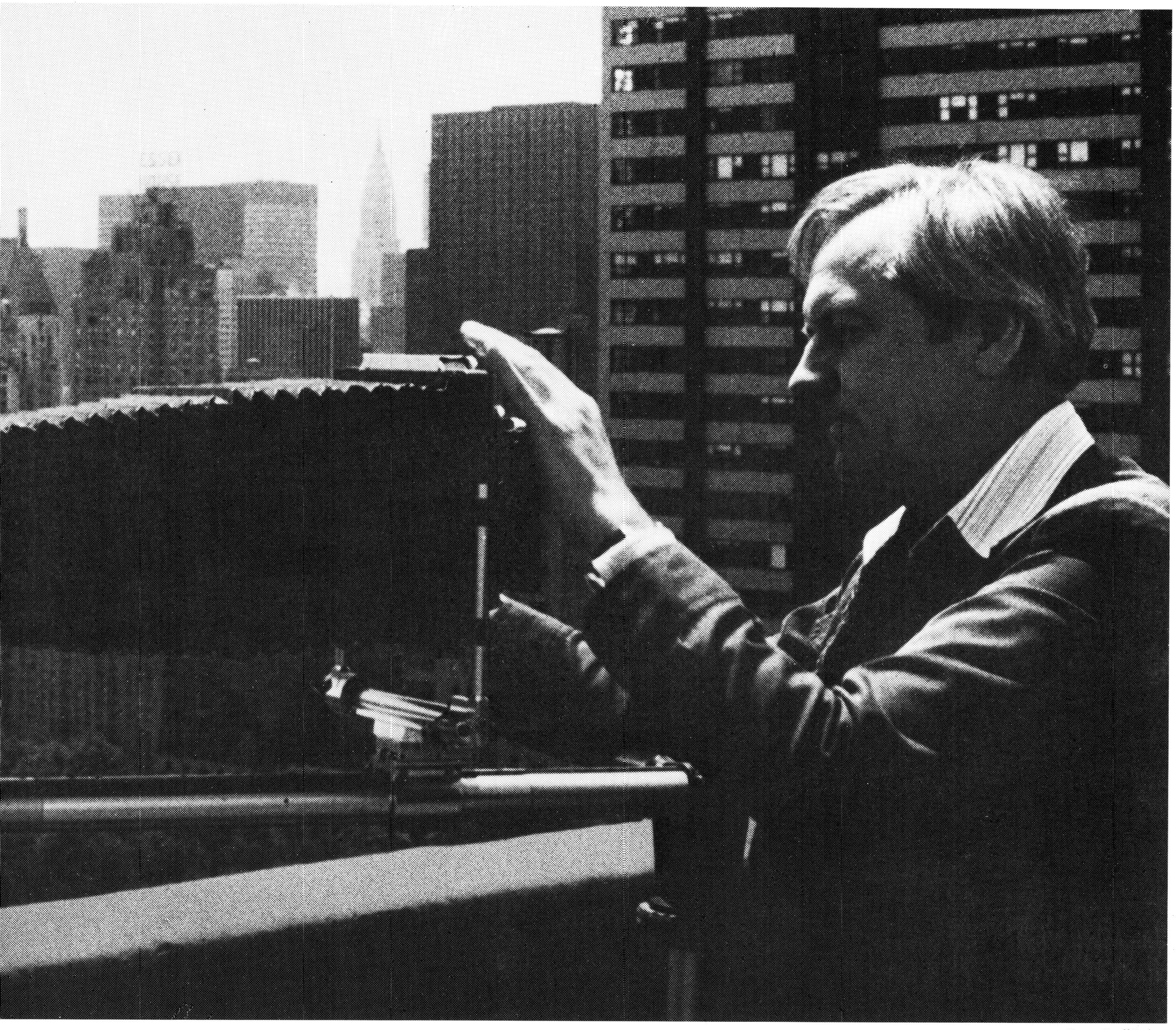

Photo: Geoff Juckes

that he wants to render and express in a picture he must first feed into it. The whole process of giving form to the photograph is thus transferred to that decisive moment before it is actually taken."

Reinhart Wolf does not photograph mere facades, he photographs "faces", lending to his silent and self-confident architectural structures something like human traits. His pictures have skintight precision, and – at the same time – an emotional reality that is palpable.

In his photographs of New York, Walt Whitman's "city of masts and spires" becomes even more visible. The shots grow from the photographer's hard struggle with this city – and with himself. They emerge from confrontations and decisions. For Reinhart Wolf it is more than the surfaces or the architecture of his subject that is important: it is the prototypical distinctiveness of this city, its peculiarly "New York" tone – the gesture of towering energy, the exaltation in stone, the thrust of buildings rocketing skyward, the dizzying superlatives – it is the very matter-of-fact presumptuousness of New York.

In the course of this photographic endeavor, in the process of taking pictures and rejecting them, in the merciless discussions we had about how the object refused to be subject – in all of this there arose that specifically "New York" tone of energy and camp, of decisiveness and devil-may-care, that gives a classic volume of photographs this visual punch that is New York.

Art does not reflect back what we see, but enables us to see, said Paul Klee.

The signature of human phantasy has been strangely engraved in these steles of capitalism. We have Reinhart Wolf to thank, this man who sees and then makes his decisions, that the inscriptions have been rendered visible to us.

The Chinese say, "Decide and the deed is already done." If that is the road to mastership, then Reinhart Wolf is already on his way.

Vilim Vasata

Reinhart Wolf is considered one the leading photographers in Europe. He was born in Berlin in 1930 as son of an architect. With a scholarship provided by the American State Department, he studied psychology, literature and history of art in USA, and later in Paris and Hamburg.

In 1956 Reinhart Wolf was awarded the degree of "Master Photographer" by the Bavarian State College of Photography in Munich. He then established his own studio for commercial photography in Hamburg. He has taught on the faculty of the College of Design and Fashion in Hamburg and has served as a member of numerous professional juries. He was a founder and past president of the Art Directors Club of Germany.

He built his Studio-Haus in Hamburg in 1969 and founded his own production company for commercials. He has been exhibiting in one-man shows in Hannover and Munich, and he has served as guest lecturer of seminars for young photographers at various universities. In 1969 he began to use an 8 x 10 inch camera to photograph buildings and other historical structures. His "Faces of Buildings", presented at the Photokina of 1976, won him wide international acclaim.

At the invitation of the Polaroid Corporation USA, Reinhart Wolf toured Georgia in 1977 and photographed buildings for another documentary series. His first book, "Faces of Buildings" was published in 1979. His editorial assignments have increasingly become a focal point of Reinhart Wolf's development as a photographer.

Both STERN and GEO magazines have commissioned work from him. In the course of several trips during 1979, Reinhart Wolf photographed the towers of New York City. The unusual results are the basis for his book.

In the same year he undertook a tour of Japan in order to photograph Japanese culinary art in pictures of great austerity and sensual simplicity. For that work he received the Gold Medal of the Art Directors Club of Germany.

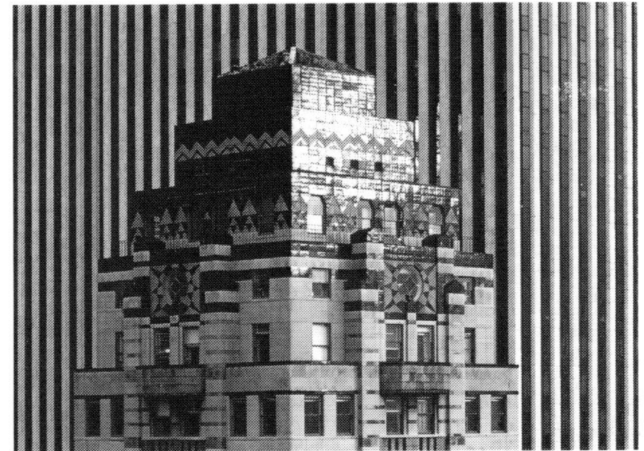

Fuller Building, 41 E./57th St., corner Madison Avenue, built 1928/29 for George A. Fuller Co. by Walker & Gillette; 42 stories, 491 feet high.

The Fuller Building was built as headquarters of the Fuller Construction Company, which was previously located in the Flatiron Building.

The Fuller Building's black and white decoration and cubic composition are comparatively stark, but its Mayan-like top, crisp elegance and glazed tiles which glisten with the gold of the rising and setting sun have made it one of the most admired art deco skyscrapers in New York.

The General Motors Building in the background, 767 Fifth Avenue, between 58th and 59th St., built 1968 by Edward Durell Stone, Emery Roth & Sons, is one of New York's least admired buildings, but here provides an interesting vertical contrast to the horizontality of the Fuller Building.

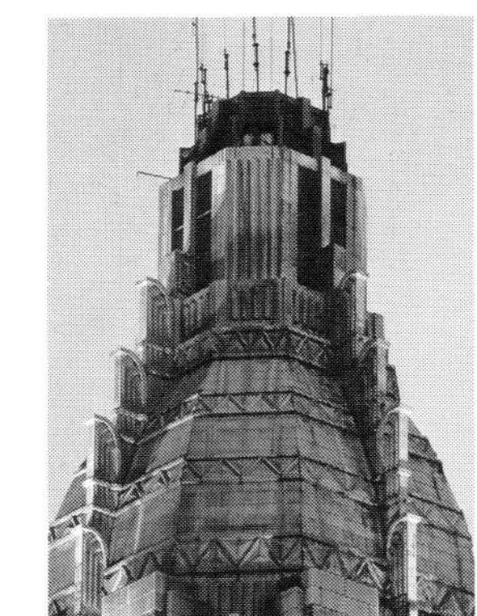

Waldorf-Astoria Hotel, 301 Park Avenue, between 49th and 50th St., built 1929/31 for Waldorf-Astoria Hotel by Schultze & Weaver; 47 stories, 625 feet high.

When the new Waldorf-Astoria opened in 1931, with its two separate apartment towers containing 500 rooms, it was the tallest hotel in the world. The old Waldorf-Astoria had been built in two sections: the Waldorf in 1893, and the Astoria in 1897, on two pieces of property on Fifth Avenue between 33rd and 34th St. owned by different branches of the Astor family.

By the 1920's the building and its location were outmoded; when the hotel moved to its present location, the Empire State Building was built on its old site.

Like most of the buildings on Park Avenue below 54th St., the Waldorf-Astoria is built on steel decking over the trainyards north of Grand Central Terminal, which became available for development with the electrification of the railroad in the early 1900's.

As with their Pierre and Sherry-Netherlands Hotels, Schultze & Weaver gave the Waldorf-Astoria a distinctive top: twin towers with a near-mansard shape broken by abstract art deco ornament. These towers mark the residential section of the hotel.

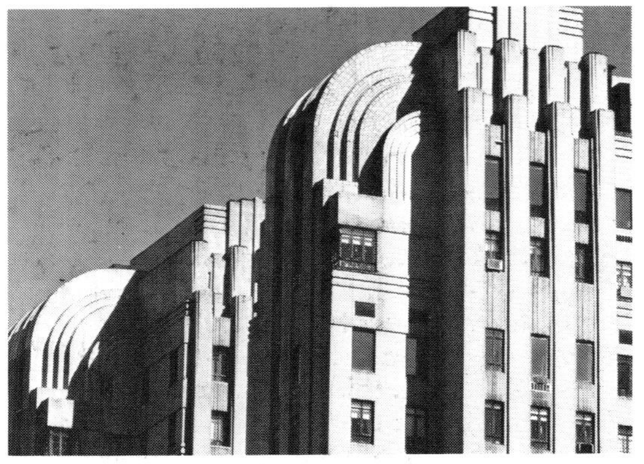

Majestic Towers, 115 Central Park West, between 71st and 72nd St., built 1929/30 for Irwin S. Chanin by the office of Irwin S. Chanin; 30 stories, today ownership apartments.

Real estate developer Irwin S. Chanin had an organization covering all phases of building: acquisition, finance, architecture, planning, construction and decoration. These were brought to bear on Chanin's best-known works, his twintowered apartment houses on Central Park West, the Majestic, at 72nd St., and the Century its near-twin, at 63rd St.

The Majestic was replanned for smaller apartments in mid-construction, as the full force of the stock market crash was being felt, and is famous for its spectacular views over Central Park and the neighboring Dakota apartment house in the north.

The rounded brickwork combines machine-age aesthetics with northern European expressionist design of the 1910's and the 1920's; it was designed for Chanin by the sculptor René Chanbellan.

The twin tower plan, which is set on a full block base, was here a response to zoning and apartment planning requirements, but later developers found the single tower plan more economic.

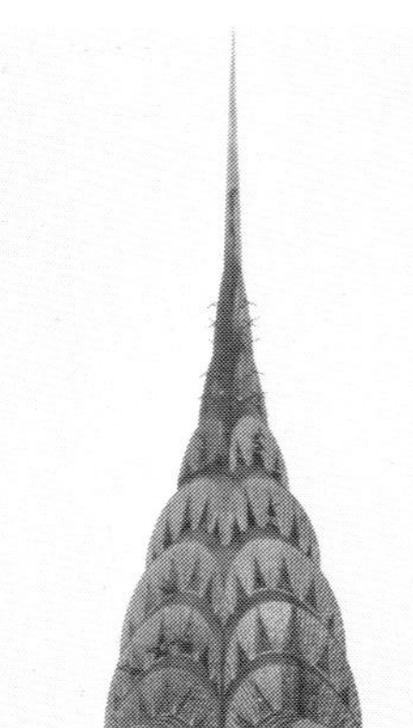

Chrysler Building, 405 Lexington Avenue, between 42nd and 43rd St., built 1928/30 for Walter P. Chrysler by William Van Alen; 77 stories, 1046 feet high.

The stainless steel crown and spire have always been considered whimsy in comparison to "serious" architecture. But even though Van Alen never prepared the manifestos of Wright, Sullivan, or Le Corbusier, this "silly" assemblage somehow continues to be the world's premier skyscraper form.

The Chrysler Building was originally planned as the Reynolds Building (after a real estate developer), to be 808 feet high, but William Van Alen increased the height when the project was taken over by Chrysler. At the same time, Van Alen's former partner, H. Craig Severance, was supervising the construction of his Bank of Manhattan Building on Wall Street, and added a flagpole to the design, bringing that building up to 927 feet, two feet higher than the announced height planned for the Chrysler Building, which would make Severance the architect of the tallest building in the world. Encouraged by Chrysler, Van Alen added the now-familiar spire in the last moments of construction, hoisting it out through the roof by a crane in 90 minutes to make the Chrysler Building the tallest in the world, at 1046 feet.

Two years later the Empire State Building, at 1250 feet, outdistanced the Chrysler Building, but Van Alen's flashy design, novel materials and last minute drama gave the Chrysler Building an enduring fame.

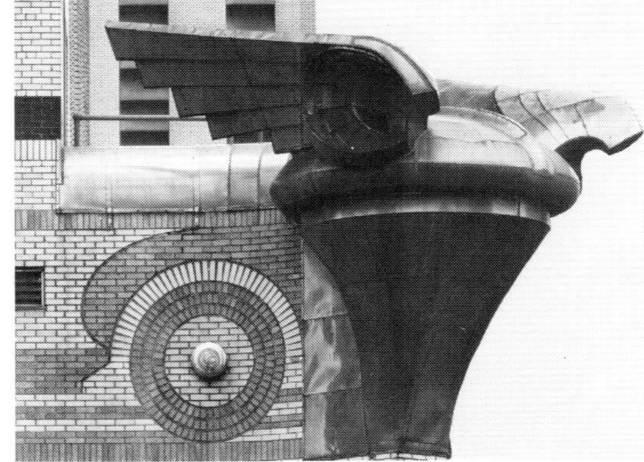

Chrysler Building, detail. Walter P. Chrysler, the founder of the automobile corporation which still bears his name, had his building decorated with symbolic designs from his cars: shown here are huge winged hood ornaments, actual hubcaps, and patterned brickwork.

In 1978 the building was designated a New York City Landmark, and is now protected from demolition or alteration.

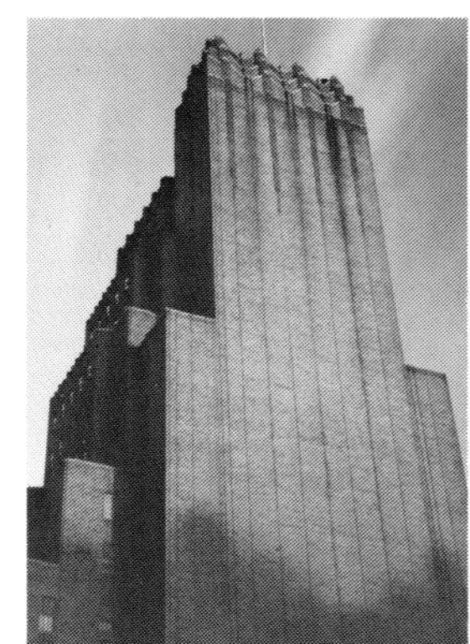

New York Telephone Company Laboratories, 207-217 W./17th St., between 7th and 8th Avenue, built 1929/30 for New York Telephone Company by Voorhees, Walker & Gmelin.

This firm designed most of the telephone company buildings in the New York area, and there are four similar buildings to this one in Manhattan.

Windowless walls have become synonymous with post World War II telephone buildings, with their automated switching equipment, but there are no windows on this facade because it conceals the elevator shafts, and is flush with a neighboring property line.

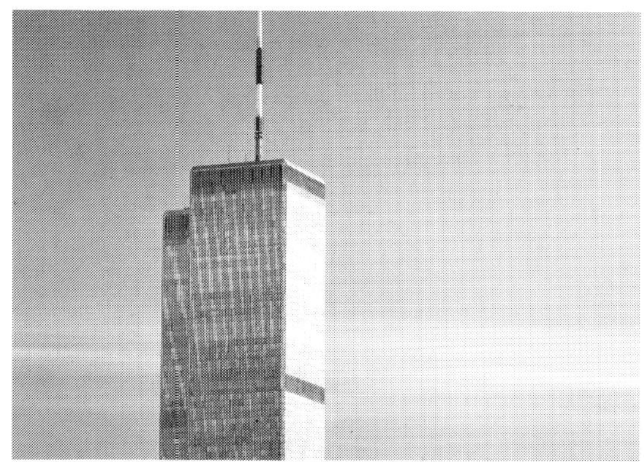

World Trade Center Towers, 10048 (zip code), Vesey, Liberty, Church and West St., built 1970/72 for Port Authority of New York and New Jersey by Minoru Yamasaki and Emery Roth & Sons; 110 stories, 1350 feet high.

The World Trade Center was built by the Port Authority of New York and New Jersey to provide centralized office facilities to organizations involved in world trade. Initially planned in the 1960's it was opposed by owners of private office buildings in the area as well as many who saw it as then Governor Nelson Rockefeller's personal but unnecessary monument.

The screen of closely spaced vertical aluminum piers recalls experiments in Gothic styling in early skyscrapers like the Woolworth Building, and eliminate the need for interior columns, except at the service core.

Most architecture critics have initially reacted with dismay to what they see as a skyline spoiled by two identical, banal boxes. Paul Goldberger writes in his A Guide of the Architecture of Manhattan: "The buildings remain an occasion to mourn, they never should have happened, were never really needed, and if they say anything at all about our city, it is that we retreat into banality when the opportunity comes for greatness."

Unlike other twin tower structures in New York city, the World Trade Center are two separate structures, not joined at a base.

Until the Sears Towers in Chicago was completed in 1974, the World Trade Center towers were the tallest in the world.

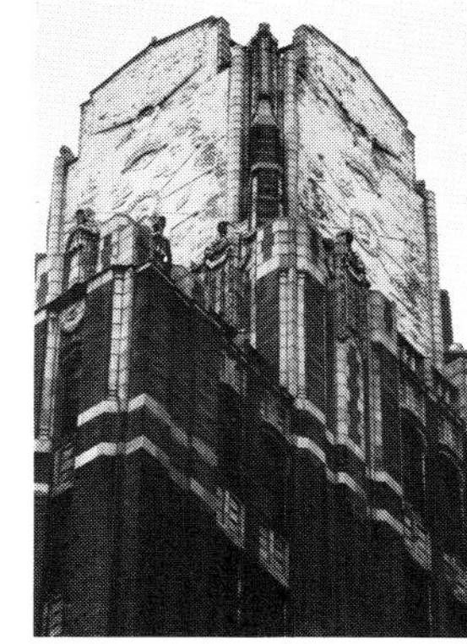

Chickering Hall, 27th/29th West 57th St., built 1923/24 for the American Piano Company and Chickering Hall by Cross & Cross; 16 stories, 220 feet high.

Chickering Hall was a combination showroom and concert hall for the American Piano Company, which absorbed the Chickering Piano Company in 1908. The water tower enclosure bears a giant replica of the Imperial Cross of the Legion d'Honneur, which was conferred on the Chickering piano by Napoleon III, and was the highest such honor ever bestowed on a piano at the time. When built, the replica was brilliantly colored and also bore the names "Chickering" and "Ampico", which have since come off. The relief portrait of Napoleon III at the center of the medial bears the circular inscription "Napoleon Empereur des Francais".

By the 1920's, West 57th Street had been transformed into a music center, with Carnegie Hall, Steinway Hall and similar institutions running from 5th and 6th Avenues. Jonas Chickering was a pioneer in the development of the upright piano in the early 19th century, and Chickering pianos are still being manufactured today. The building now contains only ordinary offices, and none of the tenants know why the Legion d'Honneur decorates their rooftop.

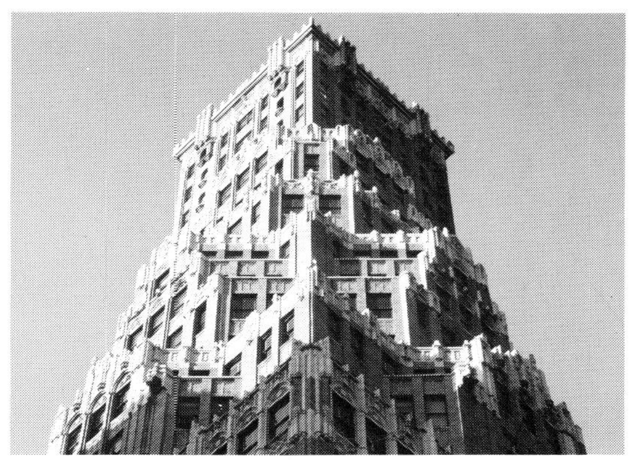

Court-Tower Building, earlier Court-Chamber Building, 66 Court St., corner Livingston St., Brooklyn, built 1926/28 for Brooklyn Chamber of Commerce by George and Edward Blum; 32 stories, 430 feet high.

The Court-Chamber Building, today being converted into cooperative apartments, assumes the classic office-loft format of the 1920's, where each floor is brought out as closely as possible to the "zoning"-envelope.

After World War II, when cost of non-standardized floor construction had risen, these setbacks were greatly simplified, as in the Look Building.

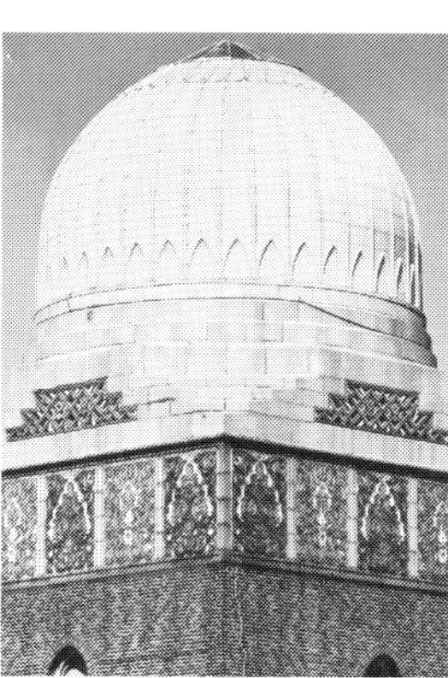

Yeshiva University, Main Building, 500 West 187th St., corner Amsterdam Avenue, built 1925/28 for the Yeshiva University by Charles B. Meyers.

Yeshiva University, established in 1897, is the oldest Jewish university in the western hemisphere, and has traditionally concentrated on Jewish religious studies. As with most other specifically Jewish buildings, the architect here adapted his work from Near Eastern sources, but the explicit use of the dome, faience plaques and the tower and minaret motifs was generally not found in the United States until the great period of eclectic experimentation which began after 1900.

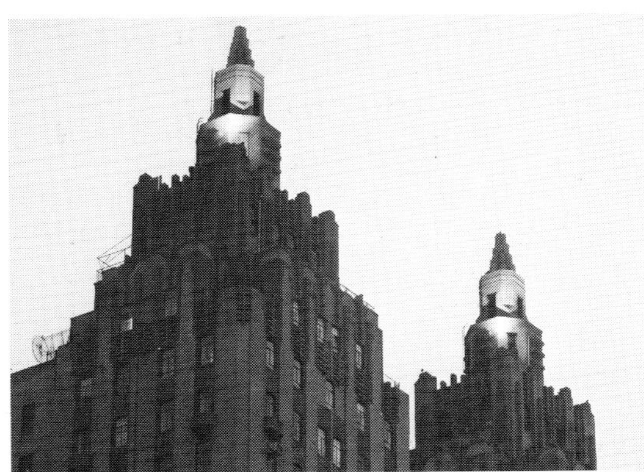

The Eldorado, 300 Central Park West, corner 90th and 91st St., built 1929/31 by Margon & Holder; 30 stories.

Like most of the full block apartment houses on Central Park West, the Eldorado was built on the site of an earlier namesake, an apartment hotel built in the 1890's which also occupied a full block front.

The distinctive pyramidal tops with two-part bases were not in the early design for the Eldorado, which was originally planned to have squared off tops.

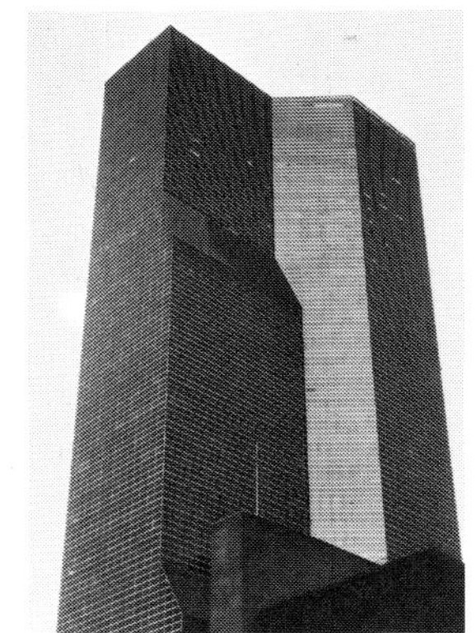

1 United Nations Plaza, 1 United Nations Plaza, corner 45th St. and First Avenue, built 1976 for United Nations Development Corporation by Kevin Roche, John Dinkeloo Associates; 39 stories, 505 feet high.

United States Mission to the U.N., 799 United Nations Plaza, corner 45th St. and First Avenue, built 1961 for Government of the United States of America by Kelly & Gruzen; Kahn & Jacobs; 12 stories.

1 United Nations Plaza is popularly known as the U.N. Plaza Hotel, even though the first 26 of its 39 floors are devoted to office space. The smaller United States Mission to the U.N., built 15 years before the hotel/office building, has a facade of blocks of concrete.

Both buildings work within a grid system which hides floor levels. Although the deep reveals of the United States Mission recall the heavy masonry systems of the early 20th century, the aluminum-glass curtain wall gives a bright elegance and an avant-garde look to the U.N. Plaza. In the background is Woodstock Tower, one of the Tudor City buildings.

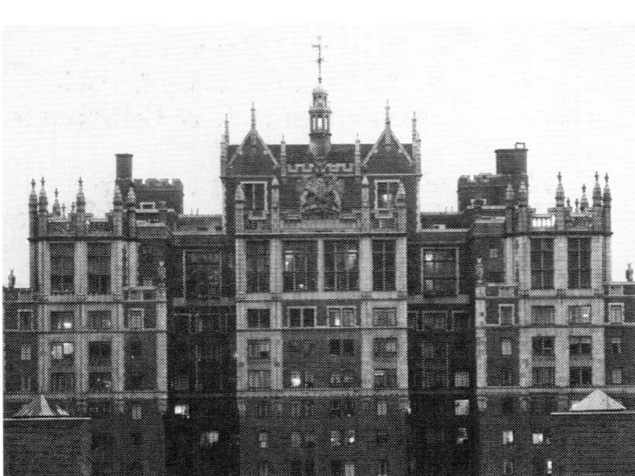

Tudor City, Middle Building, 5 Tudor City Place, built 1925/28 for Fred F. French Co. by Fred F. French Co.; 29 stories.

The Tudor City complex – 12 buildings, 3000 apartments, 600 hotel rooms – was loosely designed in the Tudor style to appeal to those who worked in midtown and wanted to avoid a long commute by subway or train. "Tudor City offers people with modest incomes a home life in beautiful surroundings..." reads an early promotional pamphlet.

It was the first high-rise urban renewal in Manhattan, planned like a small village on its town, with a park in the middle.

Despite the magnificent river views, there were very few windows on the river side, since meat-packing plants there created a disagreeable odor sometimes.

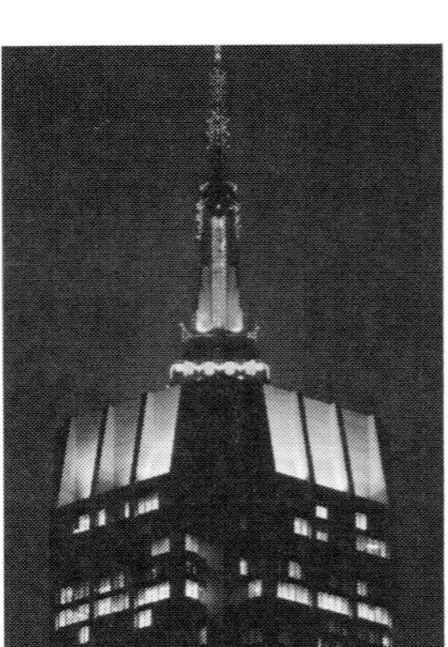

3 Park Avenue, Norman Thomas High School, 3 Park Avenue, between 33rd and 34th St., built 1976 for Educational Construction Fund by Shreve, Lamb & Harmon; 42 stories. Behind: Empire State Building.

Both buildings in this photograph – put on an optical axis and made almost one by the use of a telephoto lens – were designed by the same architectural firm, although with a time lapse of almost forty-five years.

3 Park Avenue was built as mixed-use structure containing a high school and an office building, at a time when the city was trying to develop new methods of financing school construction. Designed by Shreve, Lamb & Harmon, its mansardtype roof and tower placed at an angle to the street grid indicated a growing dissatisfaction with the effect of the standard, glass curtain wall office block on New York City's skyline, and perhaps prefigures subsequent so-called post-modern architecture.

The color lighting of the Empire State Building was begun in 1976, with the Bicentennial celebration; the first colors were red, white and blue. Today the colors change depending on national, religious or seasonal events: green for St. Patrick's Day, the Irish national holiday, blue-white for the Steuben parade in September, green-red for Christmas, yellow for Easter, orange-yellow in the autumn, red, white and blue on all national holidays and – last but not least – blue when the Yankees win.

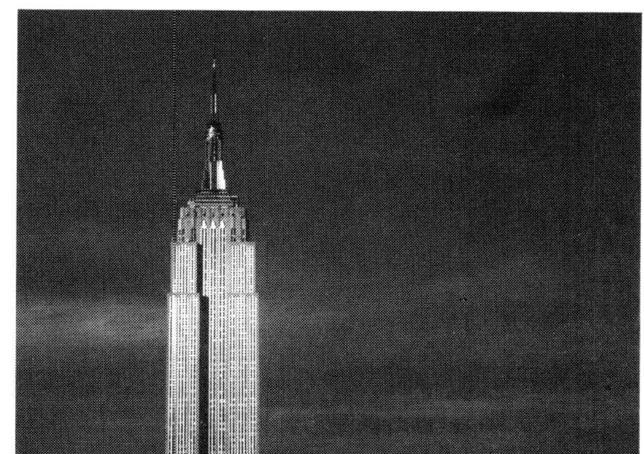

Empire State Building, 350 Fifth Avenue, corner 34th St., built 1931 for Pierre S. DuPont & John J. Raskob by Shreve, Lamb & Harmon; 86 stories of offices, 102 to top of observation deck, 1250 feet high.

The Empire State Building was the tallest building in the world until the World Trade Center surpassed it in the 1970's.

Built at the beginning of the depression on the site of the old Waldorf-Astoria Hotel, it was not fully rented until the 1940's.

Before the broadcasting tower changed its profile 1950 the Empire State Building's top was a small round half dome supposedly for the mooring of dirigibles, a use for which it was seriously contemplated.

Shreve, Lamb & Harmon went to great lengths to make the Empire State Building a machine-made structure. William Lamb wrote that "all hand work was done away with", referring to the chrome-nickel steel mullions, pre-cut limestone ashlar, and cast-aluminum spandrels. He remarked: "Whatever style it may be is the result of a logical and simple answer to the problems set by the economic and technical demands of the unprecedented program." The entire structure was completed in one year and 45 days.

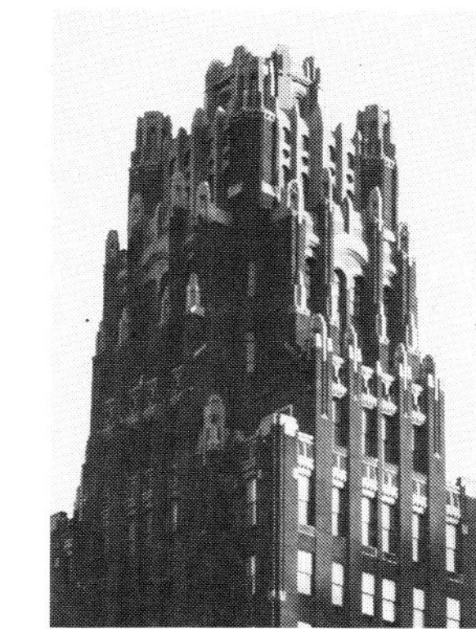

American-Standard Building, earlier American Radiator Building, 40 W. 40th St., between 5th and 6th Avenue, built 1923/24 for American Radiator Company by Raymond Hood; 21 stories, 337 feet high.

Originally built for the American Radiator Company, which manufactured coal-burning furnaces and boilers, this building was designed to represent golden, glowing embers set atop a black, charcoaled shaft.

The black brick, the first such coloring used in New York, was produced by dipping regular brick in manganese and then firing it.

This was Raymond Hood's first major building in New York, and he had been troubled by the monotony of the fenestration of the typical office building. "The windows are black holes, and the regular spacing of these black holes makes a building look like... doormats hung up to dry", he said in a 1924 interview explaining his novel design. Hood's black walls were meant to devalue the black regularity of the windows by setting them in an equally black field.

Although the American Radiator Building worked within the general format of the neo-Gothic skyscraper (like the Woolworth Building), it was advanced in its exclusive use of ahistorical decorative devices, prefiguring the shift to art deco ornament a few years later.

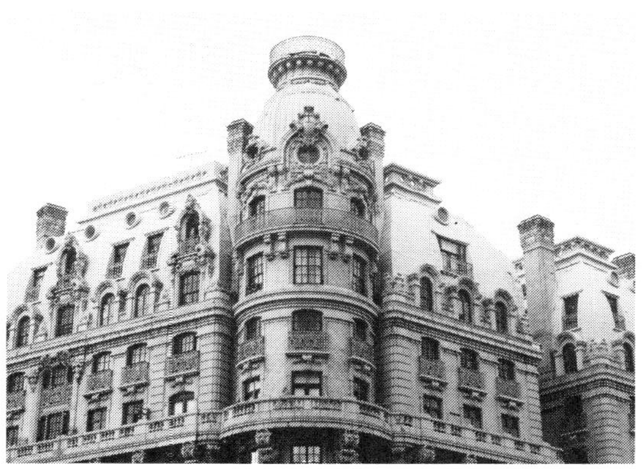

Ansonia Hotel, 2107 Broadway, between 73rd and 47th St., built 1898/1904 for William Earl Dodge Stokes by Paul E.M. Duboy & W.E.D. Stokes; 18 stories.

The Ansonia was built as a residential (rather than transient) hotel in 1898-1904 by William Earl Dodge Stokes, a prolific west side real estate developer. As a residential hotel, it is a prototype for the modern apartment house, a building type then only in its infancy.

For New York, the Ansonia's free Beaux-Arts style is unique, reflecting the novelty of multiple dwelling design in a city of private houses. "Joyous exuberance against the sky" said the official report of the city's Landmarks Preservation Commission in describing the Ansonia.

Many of the greatest names in performing arts have settled here, including Caruso, Ziegfeld, Stravinsky and Toscanini. A full block long, the Ansonia is a bit worn today, especially around its delicate roofline, but it is still one of the most famous apartment houses in New York.

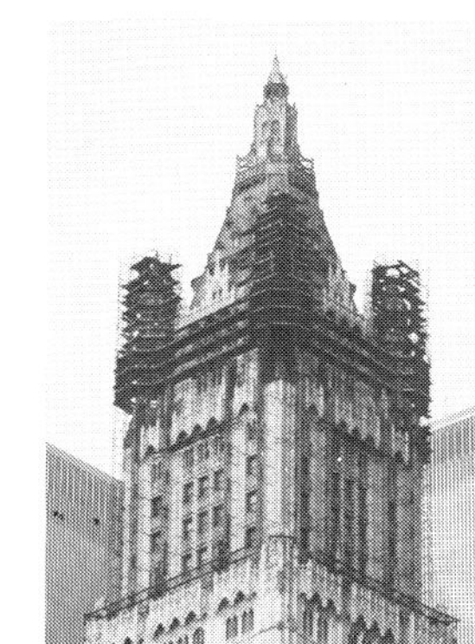

Woolworth Building, 233 Broadway, between Barclay and Park Place, built 1913 for Frank W. Woolworth by Cass Gilbert; 60 stories, 792 feet high.

The Woolworth Building was completed in 1913, and has ever since served as the headquarters of the F.W. Woolworth Company, which today operates over 2800 "5 & 10" stores worldwide. The tallest building in the world until 1930, it was built before the long term behavior of its terracotta facing was fully understood. A special fund, created by Frank W. Woolworth himself, still serves to keep the building in top condition and most of the exterior was replaced over the last three years.

The imitation of Gothic styling was much criticized by some contemporary critics, especially in Europe. Cass Gilbert, the architect, later explained "The problem of this great shaft cried aloud for some form of Gothic treatment, and the soaring sense of uplift achieved more than justifies it."

The Woolworth Building was for sixteen years the highest building in the world, until it was surpassed by Chrysler's spire. Woolworth paid for the construction of the building in cash, some $ 13,000,000, and the property has never been mortgaged.

For some time known as the "Cathedral of Commerce", its design was reportedly inspired by Woolworth himself, who greatly admired the Houses of Parliament in London.

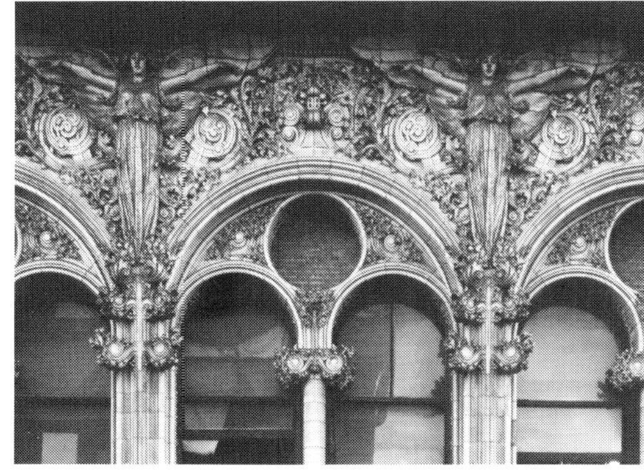

Bayard-Condict Building, 65 Bleecker St., corner Broadway/Lafayette, built 1897/98 for Silas A. Condict by Louis H. Sullivan; 13 stories.

The Bayard-Condict Building is Louis Sullivan's only work in New York, and a very early all-terracotta skyscraper.

Of the problems presented in the design of tall buildings, Sullivan wrote: "... it must be every inch a proud and soaring thing". The typical floors must be identical, but the top floor must show by "its broad expanse of wall and its dominating weight and character that the series of office tiers has definitely come to an end."

Sullivan worked primarily in Chicago and was influential on the architecture of the time through his unconventional buildings and his avantgarde writings.

The unabashed verticality of Sullivan's work was quite different from conventional, classically inspired tall buildings of the period, like the Flatiron Building.

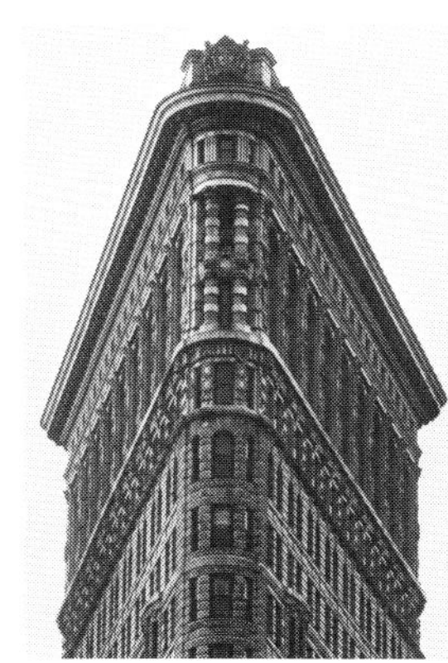

Flatiron Building, earlier Fuller Building, 175 Fifth Avenue, between 22nd and 23rd St. and Broadway, built 1901/03 for the George A. Fuller Company by Daniel H. Burnham; 21 stories, 285 feet high.

The Flatiron Building was originally named after its owner and builder, but New Yorkers persisted in naming it after its distinctive shape, which is the result of the sharp angle of crossing of Fifth Avenue and Broadway at 23rd St.

The Flatiron was an early example of a complete steel skeleton and its heavy, French Renaissance facades of limestone and terracotta were meant to allay fears about the building's stability. Although the technique of steel framing was well established by 1895, when this building was begun in 1901, people were skeptical about its future.

Several sections of the masonry wall were built from the top down, and this centrally located building must have provided firm proof to many that construction technology had made a great advance.

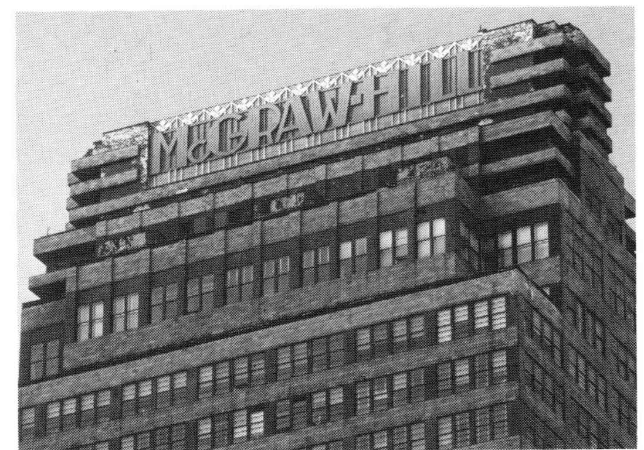

GHI Building, earlier McGraw-Hill Building, 326 West 42nd St., built 1931 for McGraw-Hill Publishing Company by Hood, Godley & Fouilhoux; 34 stories, 488 feet high.

The McGraw-Hill Publishing Company built its Headquarters west of 8th Avenue so that it could have its printing plant on-premises in compliance with zoning regulations. The result was a combination office and factory building with elements of the international, art deco and futurist styles, as well as one of the most advanced buildings of the day. McGraw-Hill was the only New York structure included in Philip Johnson and Henry Russel-Hitchcock's influential book of 1932 "The International Style".

Although stylistically influential, McGraw-Hill was not followed over to the far west side, and they vacated this building in the early 1970's for a new building on Avenue of the Americas.

Citicorp Center, corner Lexington and Third Avenue, between 53rd and 54th St., built 1977 for Citibank by Hugh Stubbins & Associates; Emery Roth & Sons; 59 stories, 900 feet high.

The silhouette of the Citicorp Center provided a "desperately needed shot of adrenalin to the city's architectural bloodstream", Paul Goldberger, architecture critic for the New York Times, has written. Indeed, Citicorp's sloping roofline was unprecedented in New York, where the flat roof syndrome was unchallenged for over 40 years. The roof was first planned for terraced condominiums, later for a solar collector, but now exists simply as a decorative shape.

The Citicorp Center also contains a technical novelty, the "Tuned Mass Damper": a 365 ton concrete block floating on oil above the 59th floor. The damper is put in motion by a computer to counteract the movements of the tower in strong winds.

Citicorp was able to build on the site only after extensive real estate negotiations with the existing property owners, including St. Peter's Lutheran Church. The church was persuaded to sell with the agreement to build a new church on the same site for the congregation, and it is now nestled between two of the four mammoth 13 stories high stilts on which the whole tower rests – right next to a subway entrance and the 6 stories high shopping atrium with stores and restaurants, where 25.000 visitors pass by daily. Part of the church is the Erol Baker Chapel of the Good Shepherd, a white oasis of peace entirely designed by the sculptor Louise Nevelson.

The tower shares some elements with modern design of the 1930's and 1940's – strip windows, aluminum panel facades, and an aerodynamic, wedge-shaped silhouette, but its silky, silvery coolness firmly places it in the 1970's.

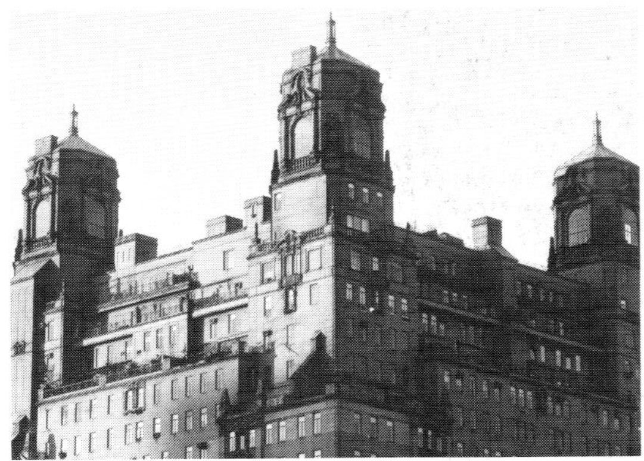

Beresford, 211 Central Park West, between 81st and 82nd St., built 1929 by Emery Roth; 22 stories.

The Beresford is one of the last of the formal, classically inspired apartment houses, a type which was nearly erased with the advent of art deco styling after 1930. With its three baroque towers, it has the bulk of a Russian fortress, dominating the corner of 81st St. and Central Park West, across from the Museum of Natural History.

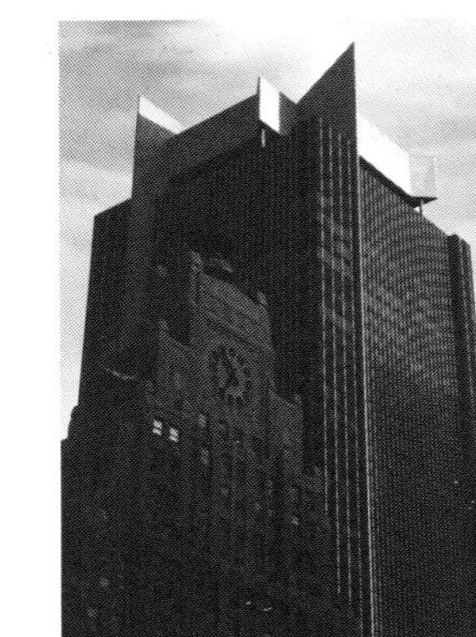

Paramount Building, 1501 Broadway, between 43rd and 44th St., built 1926/27 for Paramount's parent company, Famous Player's-Lasky Corporation by Rapp & Rapp; 33 stories, 455 feet high.

1 Astor Plaza, corner Broadway, between 44th and 45th St., built 1969/72 for Sam Minskoff & Sons by Kahn & Jacobs; 50 stories.

The Paramount Building was built in 1927 for Paramount Pictures as their production company's executive office and showcase theatre. Working for Adolph Zukor, President, Rapp & Rapp produced a simple masonry office building with classical overtones and the familiar setback required by the 1916 "zoning" resolution. The globe and clock faces at the top represented an attempt to provide a functional termination of the upper floors.

To the north, 1 Astor Plaza is built on the site of the old Hotel Astor, which it was able to commemorate only through its demolition. Built in 1969/72 by Sam Minskoff, the theatre promoter, this was the first building built under the floor area in exchange for the construction of two theatres.

The huge concrete fins and notched glass facades directly recall Frank Lloyd Wright's Price Tower in Oklahoma of 1955.

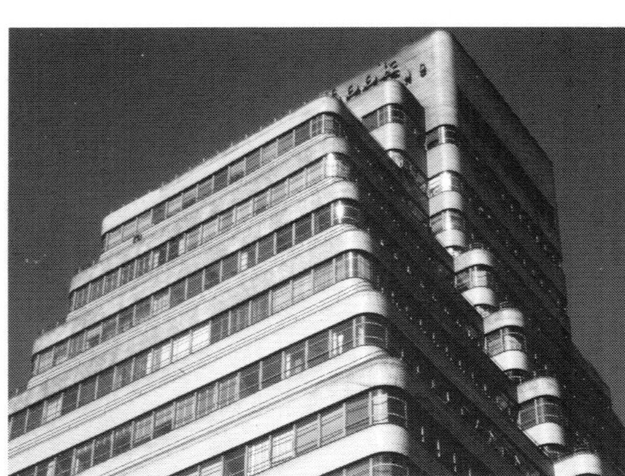

Look Building, 488 Madison Avenue, between 51st and 52nd St., built 1949/50 by Emery Roth & Sons; 23 stories.

One of the early post-war office buildings, Emery Roth's Look Building of 1950 has retained its original name long after Look Magazine has ceased to exist.

Although not the first horizontal strip windows in New York City, the Look Buildings are among the most explicit and successful. Its round corners and staggered setbacks produces a modern version of the "Look" of the 1920's.

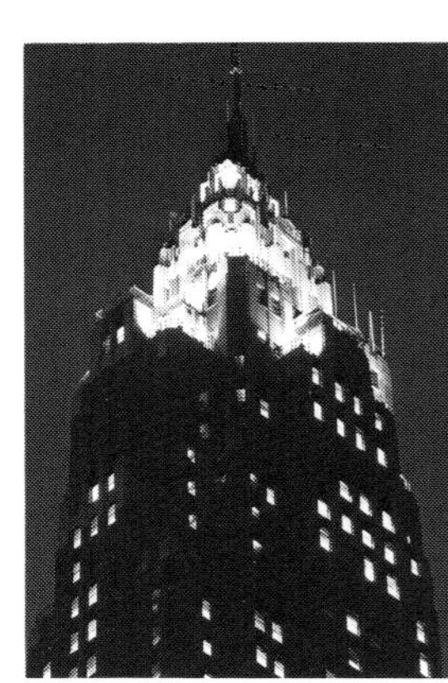

American International Building, earlier Cities Service Building, 70 Pine St., corner Pearl St., built 1931 for Cities Service Corporation by Clinton & Russell, Holton & George; 66 stories.

"New style of roof architecture which is almost sensational in its difference", or so said a promotional piece on the new Cities Service Building in 1931. The "new style" was the 35 feet cube of light at the crown, far different from the usual lantern or beacon. This building was for many years known as 60 Wall Street, even though it did not actually front on Wall; a bridge was erected to a neighboring Wall Street building to provide the cachet of a Wall Street address.

This was the first building in New York City with doubledecked elevators.

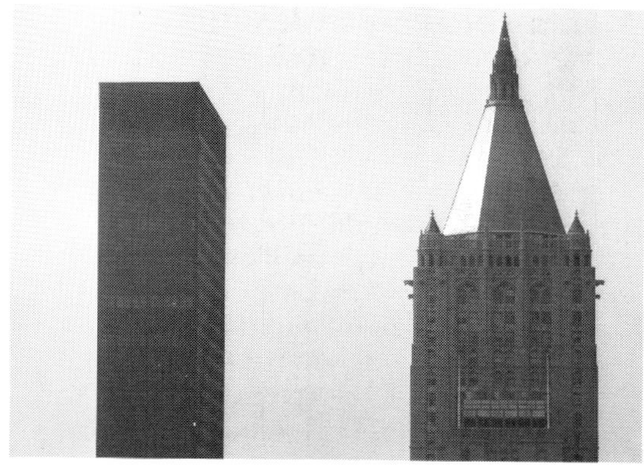

New York Life Insurance Company, 51 Madison Avenue, between 26th and 27th St., built 1928 for New York Life Insurance Company by Cass Gilbert; 33 stories, 617 feet high.

Merchandise Mart, 41 Madison Avenue, corner 26th St., built 1973 for Samuel Rudin by Emery Roth & Sons; 42 stories.

The New York Life Insurance Company building was completed in 1928 and designed by Cass Gilbert, architect of the Woolworth Building. The tower has been altered and greatly simplified but still retains its mechanical equipment under the peaked roof.

The New York Merchandise Mart was completed in 1973, designed by Emery Roth & Sons, and also has mechanical equipment occupying the top few floors. An "air rights" tower, it gained extra height by acquiring development rights to an adjacent courthouse.

Both buildings stand on noteworthy sites: New York Life demolished the old Madison Square Garden, where Stanford White, its architect, was murdered, and the Merchandise Mart tore down a designated landmark, the old Jerome mansion, the only such structure to be approved for demolition by the Landmarks Commission.

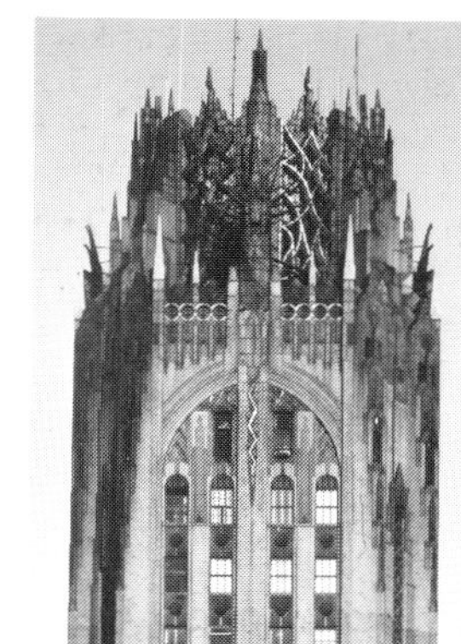

General Electric Building, earlier RCA Victor Building, 570 Lexington Avenue, corner 51st St., built 1930/31 for RCA Victor Corporation by Cross & Cross; 51 stories.

The Radio Corporation of America, a new but rapidly growing enterprise, was the original client for this richly crowned skyscraper. With its ornament of mysterious masks, whimsical copper spires and lacy, golden terracotta the building combines elements of mythology, electromagnetic radiation and art deco.

The architects used the same materials as those of the neighboring St. Bartholomew's Church: limestone and salmon-colored brick; to achieve a unified appearance between these two otherwise completely different buildings.

Later, RCA was persuaded to move into Rockefeller Center, which desperately needed a major tenant. Rockefeller Center then also tried to persuade General Electric to move to the Center, but General Electric decided against it, bought this building from RCA, and has occupied it ever since. The "gilt" masonry is actually glazed terracotta, and the ornament on top of the building is in remarkably good condition for its size and exposure.

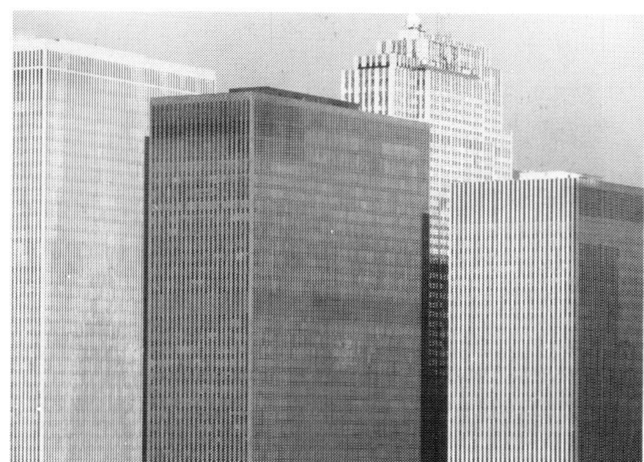

RCA Building, 30 Rockefeller Plaza, in Rockefeller Center, corner 49th and 50th St., Avenue of the Americas, built 1933 for John D. Rockefeller, by Reinhard & Hofmeister; Corbett, Harrison & McMurray; Hood & Fouilhoux; 70 stories.

Exxon Building, 1251 Avenue of the Americas, corner 49th and 50th St., built 1972 for Rockefeller Center, Inc. by Harrison, Abramovitz & Harris; 54 stories.

McGraw-Hill Building, 1221 Avenue of the Americas, corner 48th and 49th St., built 1972 for Rockefeller Center, Inc., by Harrison, Abramovitz & Harris; 51 stories.

Celanese Building, 1211 Avenue of the Americas, corner 47th and 48th St., built 1973 for Rockefeller Center, Inc., by Harrison, Abramovitz & Harris; 45 stories.

The RCA Building was and still is the centerpiece of the Rockefeller Center complex. In recent years Rockefeller Center interests have tried to build up the Avenue of the Americas into a harmonious group of towers. The Exxon, McGraw-Hill and Celanese Buildings all share the same designers and the same taut, thin vertical striping, but they do not have the setbacks or the elegant materials which give the older buildings their character.

Yet they have a subtle, successful unity and represent the only well planned office tower groupings since the 1920's.

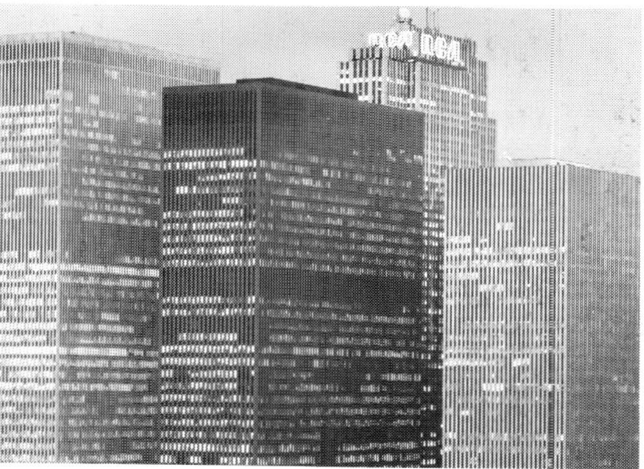

I'm greatly indebted to all who helped me with this book.
I express my thanks especially to all the doormen, superintendents and building managers who let me photograph from
the roofs of the buildings you find in this volume, to my assistant, Geoff Juckes, whose untiring research, organization
and practical help made it possible to accomplish my task, to Thomas Höpker, who got me started with an idea,
to Rolf Gillhausen, who published some of the pictures for the first time.
My thanks also to the following publishing houses: Harcourt, Brace, New York; Viking Press, New York; Random House,
New York; The New York Times Company; Gallimard, Paris; The Christian Science Monitor. The photographs were taken
in May 1979 and in February and March 1980. Camera: Sinar 8x10 inches; lenses: Rodenstock; focal lengths:
360, 480, 600 and 1000 mm. Films: Kodak Vericolor VPL, VPS and Ektachrome Daylight film.

Hamburg, August 1980
Reinhart Wolf

Translation from the German by John Woods